This is a must read for students struggling with learning challenges, the teachers who teach them, and anyone who wants to be inspired to reach their goals. Within the pages of this book, Cindy Lumpkin does a wonderful job of sharing her inspiring story to overcome a devastating learning challenge and low self-esteem in order to reveal the greatness that was within her all the time. Cindy has created a great resource in which she shares practical steps in order to take the journey of self-awareness, overcome personal challenges, and discover a better more fulfilling life.

> William O'Neal, Inspirational Speaker & Trainer
> www.williamoneal.com

DESTINED FOR SUCCESS

Cindy Lumpkin

TRIUMPH Publishing • Atlanta, Georgia

Copyright © 2005 by Lucinda Ann Lumpkin

All rights reserved. No part of this book may be reproduced, stored in a retrieval system, or transmitted in any way or by any electronic or mechanical means, including photocopying, recording or otherwise without written and signed permission from the author, except for the inclusion of brief quotations in a review.

For information address
TRIUMPH Publishing Company
5467 Jerome Road
Suite 100
Atlanta, GA 30349

or

www.triumphinlife.com

FIRST EDITION

Cover Design by John Early
www.goldeproductions.com

ISBN: 9780977862726

Library of Congress Control Number: 2007907535

TRIUMPH Publishing books are available for special promotions and premiums. For details contact: Jason Lumpkin, Director of Marketing at 770-856-1819 or Jason@triumphinlife.com

TABLE OF CONTENTS

Acknowledgments ix

Preface xi

Part I - The Educational Narrative of Cindy Lumpkin

    Chapter 1 - The Program for Exceptional Children 17

    Chapter 2 - Life as a Middle School Student 29

    Chapter 3 - A Whole New World 45

    Chapter 4 - Redefined 57

    Chapter 5 - Praise to the Women on My Journey 67

Part II - A Journey into Your Past, Present and Future

    Chapter 6 - The Individual as Reflective Explorer 79

    Chapter 7 - There is Healing in the Past 91

    Chapter 8 - Living in the Moment 107

    Chapter 9 - Charting the Course to New Horizons 117

    Chapter 10 - The Final Stop: Make Your Dreams

                   Your Reality! 129

About the Author 151

In dedication to my beloved grandfather,

Mr. Johnnie Hunt, Jr.

May you rest in peace.

Acknowledgments

First and foremost, I give honor to God. For through Him my dreams, hopes, and aspirations are possible. My faith in Him sustains me and all that I do. He has blessed me with and seen me through trails and tribulations that are now my testimonies. He gave me this vision and has allowed His glory to manifest.

This book, and in many respects the individual that I have become, would never have been possible if it wasn't for the many people I have met on this journey called life. These people are the individuals who inspired me, who showed me the ways to go and ways not to go, who believed in me and who encouraged me to continue on when I felt like giving up.

Eternal gratitude to Jason Lumpkin, supporter, friend, significant other, my man of God, who believes in me and my abilities; who supports all that my hands touch; who has been everything from my editor to designer. You complete me!

A major salute to my parents as well as John Jones for everything you have done for me. You supported my every endeavor, no matter the cost or how foolish it seemed. You sacrificed much in order that I may have and experience. I thank God for choosing you to guide me through this world. I pray that I am one day able to be the same loving parent to my children as you have been to me. Without each of you my journey would not have been the same. May God bless you.

Aunt Wolf you have been like a parent to me throughout my life; your children, Angie and Niecey, have been like my sisters. My life has been better because you have been in it. I have learned so much from each of you. Thank-you!

To the rest of my family and friends, thanks for the words of encouragement, support, and advice. I pray that each of you continue to live your dreams.

Reggie thanks for making me believe that my story is worth sharing. Yvonne and John thanks for your encouragement, talent and patience in helping me to produce this project. I could not have done it without you.

Preface

While lying down after studying for midterm exams, I began to reflect on my education, from 1988, when I was evaluated for the Special Education program at Hunterdale Elementary School, until now, 1998, my sophomore year at Virginia Union University.

I often lie awake in bed at night, envisioning new and exciting things to do, few of which I ever follow up on. What made this time different was that everything, both good and bad, that happened during my experience of the special education program came back to me with great clarity. I was astonished by all the details I was able to recall: the insensitive remarks of my peers, mistreatment by some teachers, encouraging words from others, and my moments of self-doubt. Yes, this time was different. For once, my dream was about to become a reality.

The idea nagged at me until I could no longer ignore the unknown force compelling me to start writing a history of my education. I've never felt the need to express myself by writing; in fact, writing is among my least favorite activities. Looking back now, the only reason I can think of for that need to chronicle my academic career is that I felt it might somehow liberate me from the burden of shame, self-doubt, and blame I carried through much of my education — until now…

* * *

The above episode occurred on March 6, 1998; the vision, however, seemed less vivid the next day. I convinced myself that I was incapable of following through and writing this book, telling myself, "Once again you've let your imagination run away with you." Though I had no intention then of completing the project, I could never bring myself to destroy the writing I produced that night.

I now realize that my imagination wasn't the problem. I had allowed being an individual with a learning disability to dictate my progression in life.

Three years later, on August 11, 2001, while a student at Clark Atlanta University, I was inspired to finish what it felt as though I'd begun many years earlier. The project has served several purposes. It has been an instrument to guide me on a journey to rediscover past school experiences, understand my present state of mind, and imagine the many possibilities for my future. It has allowed me to fully analyze the influence that having been in a special-education program had on my life, eventually shaping the person I've become. Perhaps most important, it has given me an opportunity to share my story and possibly change the lives of others, no matter what their circumstances, for the better.

My experiences have taught me that life is a great gift despite some of its difficult and painful conditions. It's not the fact that we have these circumstances that makes us winners or losers; rather, it's how we choose to live with them that determines whether we're successful or not.

It is my dearest hope that you use this book as a tool for personal empowerment; a guide on the most important journey you will ever take. It is the journey of getting to know yourself and overcoming life's less than optimal circumstances, whatever they may be. I invite you to make this journey with me. It will take you into your past, present, and future; it will take you through many twists and turns, highs and lows, and around some dark and scary corners. In the end, however, you will find the light — the light within you.

Part I

The Educational Narrative of Cindy Lumpkin

The Program for Exceptional Children

"Life for me ain't been no crystal stair."

This is certainly true of my life. From the very beginning, I experienced failure at school. It was never much fun bringing home frowning faces [☹] stamped on all my work. If, by chance, I did get a smiley face [☺], it was always accompanied with the phrase "Had help." I quickly learned to recognize that phrase, which meant I hadn't earned my smiley face on my own.

Unhappy with my progress for the year, my kindergarten teacher suggested to my mother that I repeat kindergarten. My mother, being the advocate she was, would not hear of it. "Kids don't fail kindergarten," she said. "Besides, she knows her

ABCs, she can count to at least a hundred, she writes legibly, and she knows all her identity information."

It was settled; I was moved along to the first grade. Though I remember little about my first year in that grade, one occasion stands out. While waiting for a conference with my teacher, my mother looked around the classroom and saw a bulletin board featuring various words, focusing on the vowel sounds. She asked me whether I knew the sounds. "A, E, I, O, U, and sometimes Y," I said. Yes, but what are their sounds?" she asked. She might as well have been speaking in a foreign language. I couldn't answer her question. She seemed disappointed in me. "You should know that, Cindy," she said, before going over each vowel sound with me.

Other than the fact that I was never assigned to a reading group and that I ended up repeating the first grade, I don't recall much more, but I do remember my second year in the first grade. I did very well, and made the honor roll the entire year. My mother was very proud of me. "I knew my baby could do it," she said.

I moved on to the second grade on my own merit, but then a new problem arose, or perhaps the same problem had just been hiding, biding its time. Suddenly, failure in school once again became a major part of my life. When I was pushed on to the third grade, school became more and more difficult for me. It was extremely frustrating.

My third grade teacher was kind; instead of failing me she placed me in the fourth grade. My report card literally read,

"Placed in the fourth grade." Just as when I was in kindergarten, I realized that the word "placed" meant that I hadn't earned the right to be in fourth grade on my own. I spent that summer with a private tutor. I'm not sure how much it helped, but I understood by then that academics just did not make much sense to me.

Thus, my journey to overcoming a learning disability began in the fourth grade, when I was referred to a special-education program. Although I did not know until the latter part of the school year that the referral process had been completed, I believe it was my fourth grade English teacher who suggested that I was a good candidate and likely to benefit from the program. For many years, I thought she had done me more harm than good. It was a long time before I realized that the very program that had contributed to my low self-esteem and confidence was in fact the program that saved my life.

I remember a woman coming into my math class that year and sitting down at the back of the room to take notes. I was unaware of it then, but with my present knowledge of the referral process, I know that she was the school psychologist. She had come into my class several times before, but this was the first time I paid attention to her. There was something distinctively different about this visit: without being told, I knew she was there to observe me. I didn't know precisely why, but I remember being on my best behavior when she came into the class.

My belief was confirmed several days later, when I was excused to accompany her to a small room in the school library, where she did a battery of tests. I looked at flip charts and, under time restraint, put together what seemed to be puzzle pieces. She also asked me a series of questions about school and my family. I never learned the results of those tests, but obviously I didn't do well. Later, I discovered that the school psychologist was also observing Lisa, my best friend. Lisa and I took a trip to the doctor's office during school hours. "Just a checkup" they said.

Lisa and I were good friends in school before we became members of the special-education program. The day we first met, Lisa was new to Hunterdale Elementary School. I introduced myself by smacking her squarely in the face! I can't remember why; I don't recall her doing anything to justify such treatment. Later, during recess, I was introduced to her sister, from whom I spent the whole time running for dear life!

I believe that God orchestrated our dynamic introduction to one another. Who would have guessed that a smack in the face would produce not just one friendship, but two? Yes, even Lisa's sister, who was a bully herself, became my very good friend.

Lisa's placement in the program helped make the transition easier for me. We would face many challenges together, but there were some that I would have to face alone. Still, Lisa was to be the motivation I needed to eventually become successfully "mainstreamed" in middle school.

Our English teacher asked Lisa and me to step outside her class, where she informed us that Mrs. Bly, Hunterdale's Special Education instructor, would be our teacher for the next academic year. We were elated to be going to the fifth grade, as Lisa had been held back twice before, and I had been held back once. Neither of us realized what our teacher meant when she said that Mrs. Bly would be our teacher that year. Still, I couldn't help remembering the psychologist's testing earlier that year, and thinking it had something to do with my new placement.

New Beginnings

All the fourth grade teachers were sitting in the hall, chatting. I stepped outside my class and asked my English teacher, "Excuse me, may I be a librarian helper?" I don't know what I expected her to say, but I figured my chances were as good as anyone else's. After all, I wasn't a bad student as far as behavior was concerned. I wasn't prepared for what she said next.

"Why, Lucinda?" she replied, "You don't do your work!"

"Oh!" I said. I looked around at the other teachers; they all giggled at me. I looked back at my teacher, who was shaking her head as if she couldn't believe I'd had the nerve to ask such a question! Embarrassed and hurt, I returned to class. I always did my work — it just never was right. "Your work is always incorrect" would have described what I produced in school; I felt it was a more appropriate assessment than "You don't do your work."

Only days before school ended, after our English teacher had talked to Lisa and me, our math teacher gave a farewell speech in which she alluded to the fact that some of us would have Mrs. Bly as a teacher the next year. Though she spoke generally, I felt she was speaking directly to me. She went on to say that, even though we were not having problems in her class, it would be in our best interest to have Mrs. Bly as our math teacher just in case we had missed something.

I felt slightly disappointed, because math and Physical Education were the only classes in which I had earned decent grades, but I dared not let the disappointment register on my face. I admired my math teacher, and didn't want her opinion of me to get any lower than I felt it already was. At that moment I felt the same way I had in the third grade, the day my Language Arts teacher caught me cheating on a spelling test and shared the news with my math teacher. I happened to have had a math test that same day, but after hearing about my cheating, my math teacher made me show her my hands. She wanted to make sure that I was not cheating in her class as well. I was deeply disappointed in myself for cheating, and unhappy at the thought that my math teacher did not trust me. She didn't understand that I would never have cheated in her class because I understood math — it was my best subject. I did not, however, understand Language Arts; words just didn't seem to make much sense to me. That would be the first of many disappointments on my long journey toward reclaiming my self-esteem.

A New Teacher

Days before school started that fall, my mother went to Hunterdale Elementary to buy my books for the coming year. When she brought them home, I was overwhelmed with joy at all the books I had. Among them were a spelling book, a science book, and a health book, as well as a history book with various leaders from the past on its cover. In addition, I had a new math book — with a peacock on it!

I took great pride in labeling a notebook for each subject. I then placed each book and notebook into my backpack with great care. The heavier my backpack, the prouder I felt. Later, I learned that I would have no use for any of those books.

I thought the first day of school was the best. I remember wearing my brand-new, pink All-Star shoes (in style at the time) and one of many new outfits my mother and I had shopped for prior to that big day. I started out wearing a hundred-dollar outfit, but by day's end, I felt like I had only a ten-cent brain to match it.

The day went smoothly at first. I met Mrs. Bly, a beautiful, petite woman who always smiled. I suspected she was older and had no kids, or that her children were already grown and out of the house by the time she became my teacher. Mrs. Bly had a way of making her students feel like she was our second parent. She always brought us snacks or toys, and was very much the expert teacher.

I met my new classmates as well, and discovered that Lisa and I were not the only students who'd been referred that year; among the others were a white girl and a black boy who had been my classmates the year before. I was quite surprised to find the white girl in my new class, because she was not the typical "at-risk student." She came from an upper-middle-class family, and her mother was president of the PTA.

That same morning, Mrs. Bly informed me that I didn't need the books my mother had bought. Seeing the disappointment on my face, she said, "I don't know why they keep doing this." She was referring to the fact the special-education students were always given books they weren't supposed to have.

She handed me three books that looked familiar. The math book was the same one I had used the year before as a fourth grader; the reading and spelling books were the same ones I had in the second grade. I was disappointed, to say the least. After all, I was an eleven-year-old fifth grader.

Reality began to set in later that day. While walking down the hall, I overheard the top-performing student in my fifth grade class say to another student, "Lucinda is in special ed. this year." When they saw me approaching them, a look of shock appeared on their faces. Though I was tremendously embarrassed, I ignored their comment. What could I say? It was true.

I soon learned that being in the elementary school special-education program wouldn't have as negative an impact on my self-esteem as it later would in middle school. Still, the reality of my situation became clearer to me; I finally realized what my fourth grade English teacher had meant the year before when she said, "You will pass, *but* you will be with Mrs. Bly."

My instruction that year consisted primarily of basic reading, writing, and math. Science, history, and health weren't part of my curriculum. I was "self-contained," which meant I spent the entire day with Mrs. Bly, except during PE and art class. The stress I had experienced in prior school years was now gone. The way was now cleared for learning and instruction on the level at which I functioned well.

Each day, for fifteen to twenty minutes, I read aloud to Mrs. Bly, who focused on the whole-language approach in teaching me to read. She also stressed phonics, but phonics made little sense to me, so learning to recognize a whole word rather than parts of it became my primary way of learning to read. I was encouraged to use context clues such as pictures or prior information to understand text.

My vocabulary increased through the use of flash cards. Every word I missed while reading was written on a flash card. That word was added to my vocabulary list, and the only way I could eliminate it from the list was to pronounce it correctly on five consecutive days. If at any time I mispronounced the word, the five days would start over. I engaged in conversation about each vocabulary word, defining its meaning and trying to make it relevant to my personal experience. My goal was to have as few words as possible in my flash-card pile. I loved reading with Mrs. Bly; for the first time, reading was a pleasure.

DESTINED FOR GREATNESS

I must admit that I grew a bit envious of Lisa as time went on, because she was "mainstreamed" (placed in regular-education) into several classes. Even so, I enjoyed much success that school year, and my mother spent more time working with me on my homework than she had in previous years. Each night we would go over the material in my reading book, study my spelling words, and do whatever math homework was assigned that day. I started to enjoy school a little more, and even started to like doing homework, particularly the daily reading assignments.

My mother would read a page in my reading book first, after which I would read the same page. She encouraged me to follow along as she read, and to mimic her tone and the way she paused after each punctuation mark. If I did not read as smoothly as she knew I could, I had to repeat the process. Mother then asked me questions about what we had read, and defined any words in the text that I had problems with. The combination of my mother and Mrs. Bly's patience and instruction helped me greatly improve my reading by the end of that year.

Despite being self-contained, I showed signs of promise of being able to compete with my regular-education peers. During the spring semester, all the fifth grade students participated in a program called D.A.R.E. — Drug and Alcohol Resistant Education. Once a week, a local police officer came to class and instructed us on the importance of not using drugs and alcohol. At the end of this training, each student had to write an essay on drugs and alcohol. Three essays were selected, and the writer had the privilege of reading his or her essay at the formal D.A.R.E. ceremony.

I worked hard on my essay all weekend, and accomplished the task by myself, with the exception of needing a few misspelled words corrected. The title of my essay was *Self-destruction*. From my perspective at the time, I explained that drugs had once been used as painkillers for wounded soldiers. Over the course of time, however, people became addicted, and drugs began to be used for pleasure. I ended my essay with the following: *If you use drugs and alcohol then you are headed for self-destruction.*

Boogie Down Productions' popular song "Self Destruction" influenced my essay, and, like the song, the essay was a hit. I read it at the ceremony in front of my entire fifth grade class and our families and friends. Their enthusiastic response boosted my self-esteem. No one knew it, including myself, but my ability to write and deliver such a profound motivational work was a glimpse into the future of a little girl who was diagnosed as learning-disabled.

LIFE AS A MIDDLE SCHOOL STUDENT

The prospect of starting middle school was exciting. I knew that I'd miss Mrs. Bly and the caring environment she created, but advancing to middle school was a rite of passage that all students anticipated joyfully, and I was no different. I looked forward to attending Southampton Middle School.

Those feelings were short-lived! A week before school began, I found out that I would be in exploratory classes instead of in the band class I'd requested. I can still feel the sting of disappointment I experienced as my eyes scanned the schedule, which I thought was my new beginning. There was no indication of my expressed desire to participate in the band, and I accepted it, because I didn't know I had any options.

HIGHS AND LOWS

Life in middle school is an emotional roller coaster, and this already taxing phase is further complicated for a special-education student by realizing the difference between oneself and one's regular-education peers. This was a most traumatic point in my academic career; a turbulent period during which my peers began wondering why they only saw me at physical education class, and why I, a sixth grader, had lunch with the eighth grade students. It was also at this point that I started to feel the embarrassment that usually comes along with being labeled "special."

Being a sixth grade student in special education was one big disappointment after another. I didn't eat lunch with my sixth grade peers, I was in a special-education homeroom, band class was removed from my schedule, and I was unable to tour Union Camp with the rest of my sixth grade classmates.

Union Camp, now International Paper, is a huge corporation in Franklin, Virginia, my hometown. Every year, the sixth grade class was invited to tour the company's facilities. I found out about the tour from Lisa, who now had only two special-education classes and was therefore in a regular-education homeroom. I was still self-contained (entirely in special-education classes). Lisa asked if I had turned in my permission slip to attend the field trip; she described the details of it and told me that it was for all sixth graders.

I knew nothing about the trip, but if it was for sixth graders then I was interested in going. I asked my homeroom teacher about it. She was unaware of the trip, but told me I should speak with someone in the office. I explained the situation to the principal, who told me that my homeroom teacher would have to give me a permission slip.

"Who's your homeroom teacher?" he asked.

I told him and he said, "Oh, I see. I apologize, but that homeroom wasn't given the information."

"But I am a sixth grader," I said.

"I do apologize, it was a mix-up on my part," he replied.

"Well, may I have a permission slip so that I can go?" I asked.

"We had to inform workers at Union Camp exactly how many students would be participating. That information was turned in two days ago and the trip is tomorrow. I will make sure this doesn't happen next year," he said.

I thanked him, and, as I walked out of the office, I thought, *A lot of good it will do me next year. I'll be a seventh-grader then.*

I never got to tour Union Camp.

LIFE IN THE DUNGEON

The bell rang, signaling the change of classes; however, I remained, and many of my classmates chose to join me. I refused to let anyone see me leaving or entering "the dungeon."

Aptly named by my regular-education peers, the dungeon, was a section of a building used for special-education classes. The name fit the old, dark, dingy building well. It is difficult to explain its architectural character, but it was a smaller building separate from the main one. It housed three classes: an art class that was located high in the upper level, and two special-education classes located on the lower level at the back of the building. An opening connected the two special-education classes, but the door connecting the art class to the special-education classes was boarded shut. I was grateful for the privacy, as were my classmates.

On those occasions when I had to venture outside the walls of the dungeon, I did so very carefully, trying not to draw attention to myself. My efforts were futile; people often noticed me. There was no way to escape the intrusive eyes of my peers. Common sense should have told me that, especially as I knew that there was a regular-education classroom housed in an outdoor portable located in front of the dungeon. Still, this didn't prevent me from running and ducking in and out of my classroom to avoid the piercing gaze of my fellow students. I even risked being tardy, waiting until all the others had entered their classrooms before running into my own. Those infractions eventually accumulated, and my teacher wrote me a referral to the office. I viewed it as a small price to pay to keep my secret. Deep inside, I knew that the other students knew, but I felt safer pretending they didn't.

Cindy Lumpkin

The Worse of Two Evils

It was extremely painful to deal with the stares and disapproving looks and words of other students, but the biggest blows came from teachers. Some seemed deliberate, while others simply resulted from ignorance. I realized later that it was the behavior of some of my teachers that had the most negative impact on my self-worth and self-confidence regarding academic performance.

One of the first incidents I encountered was in my sixth grade Health/P.E. class. I liked the teacher and I knew he thought highly of me as a student because I worked so hard in his class — even then, my work ethic was evident.

One day, he gave us an assignment and, as usual, the majority of the class complained. I got straight to it, however, because I wanted the freedom to play basketball, as he promised I could after completing the work. He often used free time to motivate students to complete their assignments, and it always worked for me! When I handed him my completed assignment, he didn't give his usual immediate consent to play basketball. Instead, he looked at me, a disbelieving frown on his face, and said, "You're in special ed?!"

The question shocked me. I thought he had known. I was so surprised I that I couldn't answer him. I slowly nodded a yes, turned, and walked away feeling deeply ashamed. His reaction to the discovery confirmed for me the fact that being in special education was bad.

After this episode, I grew even more confused. I was embarrassed to know that someone who obviously hadn't known my secret before knew it now, and I couldn't understand why the teacher found it so hard to believe that I was in special education. Clearly, he thought I was too bright to be in the program. All I could think was *If I'm so bright, or even average, then why am I in a special-education program*?

Incidents such as this motivated me to work harder to get out of special education. I hated being there; moreover, I hated how I felt about myself. I saw no benefit in being in special education, so I immersed myself in schoolwork, trying to prove that I could function in regular-education classes.

Moving Forward

By the end of sixth grade, I had mustered enough courage to ask my teacher, Mrs. Bailey, if she could "mainstream" me in math class. To my surprise, she said yes, but what followed gave me the extra drive to show her I could handle it: "Don't you embarrass me," she said.

Mrs. Bailey meant that she was putting her credibility on the line by mainstreaming me. She didn't want me to make her look bad by failing, and she didn't want to suffer the backlash from the regular-education teacher if I did. I took no offense at her admonition — I was so grateful to be mainstreamed that nothing anyone said could have offended me.

The next year, in seventh grade, the other special-education teachers at Southampton Middle School, Mrs. Jones and Mrs. Tucker, became my teachers. This was truly a blessing from God, because these two were the opposite of Mrs. Bailey; they were true advocates for me and for my classmates. Still, all of their support and guidance wasn't enough to protect me from the insensitive actions of their fellow instructors.

Thanks to Mrs. Tucker, I finally became a member of the band. One day I was talking with one of my special-education classmates who was in the band. I wanted to know how he'd been able to get in while I could not. I had always thought that my change of schedule was due to the "Special Education" label I carried.

Mrs. Tucker must have overheard that conversation, because she asked me a couple of questions about the situation. She then explained that I could be in the band if I wanted to. She made the necessary additions to my IEP (Individualized Education Program) and the rest was history!

Once I got into band class, I had to decide what instrument I wanted to play. For me, that was the easy part; I wanted to play the drums, like my brother did. When I told my choice to Mrs. Hill, the band teacher, she politely said, "Well, Lucinda, won't you try the clarinet? Do you know Ann Hamilton?"

"Yes," I said.

Ann was a special-education student who was several years older than I. She had learned to play the clarinet well, had played in the school band, and continued to play throughout high school. Apparently, Mrs. Hill's reasoning was that if Ann could learn to play the clarinet, then so could I. Well, Mrs. Hill was totally off base: the clarinet worked well for Ann, but not for me. I stunk at playing it!

Though I don't regret not learning to play the drums, I often wonder how I would have progressed had I tried. Might I have learned to play as well as my brother did? Would I have found it as exciting as he did? Would I have developed a love for the drums and continued to play throughout high school? These questions will remain forever unanswered, because, as a result of the special-education label, my individuality was never considered. It wasn't that when Mrs. Hill saw me she saw Ann; the issue was that she saw only a special-education student.

As it turned out, learning to play the clarinet was a great experience. I could have learned to play a lot better than I did if I'd practiced every night, as Mrs. Hill asked all her students to do, but I just didn't have a passion for it. Other than wanting to be like my brother, my reason for participating in the band was because it made me feel like a regular student. I never had to worry about who saw me entering and exiting the band room; in fact, I wanted people to see me going into band class. I was thrilled about going to class each day, though I wasn't excited about playing the clarinet or hearing Mrs. Hill scold me for not practicing. But that was a small price to pay for feeling "regular" — not special — just regular.

FOR SOME KNOW NOT WHAT THEY DO

Mrs. Hill's wasn't the only class in which I felt regular. I felt the same way in Mrs. Baskin's math class — the one in which Mrs. Bailey had told me not to embarrass her. I remembered Mrs. Bailey's words every day while attending Mrs. Baskin's class. I got off to a slow start, but I worked hard and eventually got the hang of it.

I was even more excited about Mrs. Baskin's class because, contingent on my behavior, I could earn points toward a prize from Mrs. Jones and Mrs. Tucker's behavior-modification program. My behavior had never been a problem, so I never had reason to think that Mrs. Baskin would hesitate to verify that I had earned my points for the day. Apparently, however, she had a problem with her participation in the program.

One day after class, as I had done many times, I went to Mrs. Baskin's desk and asked her to initial the slip of paper verifying my having earned that day's points. She began to rant about how tired she was of having to initial the slip of paper each day. Her rage hurt and embarrassed me, because I had done nothing wrong and couldn't understand what had made her respond to me in so cruel a manner. Worse, she had done it in front of a classroom visitor whom my family and I knew!

I responded as I did in every situation that hurt my feelings — I cried. Although I had dried my tears before entering Mrs. Jones's room, she knew something was amiss.

"What is wrong, Lucinda?" she asked. I didn't want to talk about it. I just wanted to forget the incident, but eventually I explained what had happened. Judging by Mrs. Jones's facial expression, she wasn't happy.

"You don't have to ask her to sign your slip ever again," she told me, and then muttered something under her breath that I wasn't able to understand. I knew, however, that she was on my side and that she didn't condone Mrs. Baskin's tirade. Not surprisingly, Mrs. Jones and Mrs. Tucker's behavior-modification program became extinct shortly thereafter.

Despite Mrs. Baskin's lack of cooperation, I did well in her math class, especially considering that it was my first mainstream course since having begun the special-education program. That success was largely due to Mrs. Jones, who, whenever I needed help, was always willing to explain or repeat. She never gave the work for her own class precedence over my work for other classes, nor adopted the attitude that we couldn't do my math in her science class. She made the time for whatever I needed help with during science class.

I ended up earning a "C" in Mrs. Baskin's math class that year. That grade proved that I had the ability to function with my regular-education peers.

Going On

Any doubts Mrs. Tucker and Mrs. Jones may have had about whether I could be successfully mainstreamed were erased by my performance in Mrs. Baskin's math class: they added English to my mainstream classes for the eighth grade. I, on the other hand, needed more convincing.

The next year, in eighth grade, I was elated: for the first time since elementary school, I was in a regular-education homeroom and finally got to eat lunch with students in my own grade, which did wonders for my self-esteem. I was now taking only two special-education classes, not including study hall. I was still unsure of myself, but proud of the strides I had made, and despite my anxieties, looked forward to English class with optimism.

I was very pleased to find that Lisa was in my English class. She had gotten entirely out of the special-education program the previous year. I felt much more comfortable knowing she was seated next to me. Looking back, I realize now that it was Lisa who most inspired the desire I developed to shun the label of "special."

The first day in English class was unforgettable. The teacher began by distributing books, after which she asked, "Who can name the eight parts of speech?"

None of my classmates raised their hands. I couldn't believe what I was witnessing. I thought I must have heard her incorrectly, because there was simply no way that I could know an answer that my classmates, all regular-education students, didn't. When no one responded, she said, "I know there's someone here who knows the eight parts of speech."

I was afraid, but raised my hand. She acknowledged me and I proceeded to recite the parts of speech correctly. She praised me, and then continued the lesson. I was bewildered, unable to understand why my classmates couldn't answer that simple question. My concentration was shot for the remainder of the period.

The rest of the school year went much the same way. I was amazed at how much I knew and was able to retain compared to my regular-education classmates. Despite not being a great reader or speller, I was one of the top students in English class. Here I was, a special-education student who out-performed most — if not all — of the students in my regular-education English and math classes. It just didn't make sense to me. It would be a very long time before I accepted the fact that I was just as bright as the average student, even if I had a learning disability.

The success I enjoyed that year was due in large part to Mrs. Jones and to my own determination. I had resource period with her during the same time she was scheduled to teach science to eight other self-contained students who were on varying levels and in different grades. Its amazing how she was able to manage a class of such diverse ability levels and yet find time to revisit various math concepts and language arts and reading skills with me. After she had taught her lesson for the day, or started her students on their class work, she would work one-on-one with me. The skills and methods she taught would serve me all the way through high school, college, and graduate school.

Mrs. Jones quickly identified a lack of organization as a hindrance to my learning. My notebook and notes more closely resembled chatter than they did the information my teachers tried to impart in their lessons. Mrs. Jones helped me become organized by showing me how to divide the notebook for each class into different sections, and taught me a color-coding system using highlighters. Thereafter, information started to make more sense to me, and studying my notes was easier using the new system she helped me develop. I quickly learned to distinguish between what was important information and what wasn't. By the time I got to college, I was a superb note taker. The rough draft of my notes was always sloppy and riddled with misspelled words, but once back in my room, with spell check, dictionary, and highlighters, my notes became a masterpiece. I learned later that repetition — writing and rewriting my notes — helped me to more fully absorb information. In essence, as a result of what Mrs. Jones, Mrs. Bly, and Mrs. Tucker taught me, and the methods I developed along the way, I learned how to learn.

A Good Teacher is Priceless

I have been blessed beyond belief in regard to the people who taught me, particularly in the early years of my education. Some of my teachers left a lot to be desired regarding the art of teaching young minds, but their negative attitudes and actions would never overshadow the positive influence of a wonderful few. Life would have been very different for me were it not for three excellent teachers who prepared me for the brilliant educators whom I would eventually meet in Southampton High School, Virginia Union, and Clark-Atlanta University.

When I compare myself to students who were or are in situations similar to my own, I often wonder if they had teachers who were advocates for them and pushed them to dare to believe the unbelievable. I believe that the scarcity of such teachers accounts for the low success rate among students with learning disabilities. It is not that these students lack the ability to perform well, but that they don't get the appropriate support from their educators and, in some cases, from their families during the most crucial period in their lives — the middle school years.

As I reminisce on that time in my life, I can understand why I was confused: I got so many mixed messages from key teachers who questioned my academic ability; as a result, so did I.

The most notable of these teachers was my eighth grade math teacher, Mrs. Trigg. I performed outstandingly in her class. I was her top student, which was confirmed at the end of the year at the academic awards assembly. I received the certificate for the highest grade-point average in her math class. Even though I made the grade, she still doubted my ability.

The annual Math/Science Fair was held every spring. I did my project on the metric system. I received an honorable mention, which was less than I needed to advance to the next round of judging. I was allowed to attend the fair at the next level, but wasn't allowed to compete. My classmate, Kathy, who did not place at all, was also allowed to go. I remember asking Kathy why she was able to attend the fair. I knew it wasn't because of her project entry. She said, "Mrs. Trigg asked me to take the eighth grade math test." (This was a competition in itself.) Kathy then said, "I don't know why she didn't ask you; you do so much better in her class than I do."

I realized the truth of her statement, but also realized why my teacher hadn't asked me to take that test: it was because I still had the "Special Education" label. She simply didn't have confidence in me, which hurt, but I felt I understood why she had made her decision. I often made excuses for teachers who questioned my ability to achieve academically — and I actually found myself believing them.

Discovering a New Dimension of School

Despite the negativity I endured, there were positive aspects to my middle school years, including an introduction to the glorious world of organized sports. Playing sports became my refuge and among the best decisions I made in the eighth grade. Not only did I enjoy playing on the basketball and volleyball teams, but I also felt equal to my fellow students. I hadn't had that feeling since entering the special-education program.

Athletics entailed no pressure to read and write well, although maintaining a high GPA was stressed nonetheless. All I had to do was listen, watch, and demonstrate my mastery of a given technique by shooting a basketball or spiking a volleyball. Even when I couldn't do this to my coaches' satisfaction, there were no negative repercussions, and the coaches didn't behave as though they thought I was unintelligent.

I was a sight to see while first learning to spike a volleyball! My timing was nowhere near what it needed to be to spike the ball successfully. I would take a spiking approach, swing with all that was in me, and miss the ball entirely, striking nothing but air. Even though my skills weren't so good at first, there was no harm done. The technique was simply demonstrated over and over, and practice was implemented until the intended result was achieved. Sports came easier to me than academics did; I often asked myself why education couldn't be as simple.

A Whole New World

The 1992–93 year at Southampton High marked a fresh start in my education and my life. I was more outspoken, confident, and ready to put the unpleasant scholastic experience of the past behind me. Two weeks before school started, I received my schedule in the mail. As I read it, I could have sworn that history was repeating itself. Just as when I was about to start the sixth grade, I was again disappointed. I had requested placement in Algebra I, but had been placed in a Math 9 class instead. This time, I determined not to keep quiet about it.

My mother was my saving grace — she supported me in all I did, and this time was no different. She took me to school to talk with the guidance counselor about my class schedule. I was ready to fight tooth and nail to get my schedule changed, but the guidance counselor for ninth and tenth grade students was a lovely woman, and, to my surprise, none of that was necessary. She simply explained that I had been placed in Math 9 because of my score on a pre-test I had taken during school orientation.

She pulled my file, read it, and said, "You passed the test, but with a low score." When she told me that it was ultimately my decision whether to take Algebra I, I elected to take it. My mother wrote a note confirming that I had her permission to take the class, and the situation was resolved. With that taken care of, I was ready to start my high school career on my terms — or so I thought.

Beginning Again

On the first day of school, I got a rude awakening. During homeroom, my teacher passed out several new schedules. As I read over mine I saw two changes. The first and most crucial was my English class, which had been changed from one taught by a ninth grade regular-education English teacher to a class taught by Mrs. Ward, a special-education teacher. I didn't want the watered-down education that I felt the special-education program was sure to provide. I didn't want to just get by. I still had something to prove to myself, so I expressed my feelings to Mrs. Ward. She tried her best to convince me to stay in her class, essentially telling me that I would fail in any other English teacher's class. This infuriated me.

I wondered if her insistence on my staying in her class was borne of genuine concern. Perhaps it was, but I decided I simply couldn't stay. After hearing her stories of the students who'd ended up right back in her class, I almost reconsidered, but the negativity I felt toward the special-education program ran deep; I wanted nothing more to do with it. Only later would I fully understand that the program wasn't the problem; rather, it was the way people viewed the students in Special Ed.

The other schedule change was that instead of having study hall with the regular-education students, I was with Mrs. Vick, the resource teacher. I wasn't happy with this change either, but I reasoned that it wouldn't be wise to refuse valuable help, and besides, it was only study hall.

For the most part, the decision to stay with Mrs. Vick was a good one. She was very kind and helpful, but, like many of the teachers I had encountered, she had no faith in my ability to succeed in regular-education classes. I knew it wasn't personal, but rather that I had already been marked as lacking the academic ability of "normal" students.

During the first week of school, I recall being in study-hall class and asking Mrs. Vick if she could explain something to me. She was pleased to help until she saw that it was algebra with which I needed a hand. She became instantly annoyed, and I understood why: she thought I was incapable of succeeding in that class.

"Why do they keep putting you guys in these classes?" she said.

"Well," I replied, "I'm pretty good at math and I elected to take Algebra I." I told her that I had received the award for the highest grade-point average in my "regular" eighth grade math class. She then explained what I needed to know about my homework, but from that day forward I kept my questions to a minimum.

By the spring semester, I decided that it was time to cut my ties with the special-education program. I had excelled in all my classes, had even received A's in many of them, but was still a bit unsure of my continuing ability to perform. Once again, my desire to be seen as "regular" overshadow any other feelings I had.

It seemed that at every turn someone was questioning my ability, not because I had given them any reason to do so, but because of that persistent label. This became even more apparent when an assistant secretary was appointed to assist me after my fellow students elected me to serve as secretary of our ninth grade class. At first, the reason didn't cross my mind, but after observing that no other class had an assistant secretary, I realized that the decision had been made because I was an individual with a learning disability. It was easy to believe; after all, Mrs. Ward, the special-education English teacher, was the advisor to the ninth grade officers. She was fully aware of my special-education position. Not much was expected of freshman class officers, but because of my LD status, it was assumed that I was incapable of carrying out my duty as class secretary.

Nevertheless, having endured the special-education program, I made a complete turnaround. My self-esteem and confidence shot through the roof, and I began to make significant academic progress. Many of my fellow students had forgotten, or seemed not to care anymore, that I had ever been in Special Ed. They now saw me as a leader, and, as a result, I started seeing myself as one. I became increasingly involved in extracurricular activities, and held office in many of the organizations in which I was a member.

Despite my progress, some people remained skeptical. They were not my peers, who, in fact, seemed to have more faith in me than I had in myself. Though they regularly voted me into positions of responsibility, I continued wondering if I'd have to prove my abilities to others for the rest of my life. Fortunately, things did get better. I was recognized during the awards ceremony at the end of each school year. During my last four years at Southampton County public schools, I enjoyed so much success that by my senior year I had a 3.3 GPA, was ranked eighteenth in a class of 165, and would soon receive a diploma bearing the governor of Virginia's seal of academic excellence. I had also earned a number of awards for athletics and academics.

After winning at the local and district levels, I earned the right to represent the state of Virginia in FHA (Future Homemakers of America) Star Events. The school financed a week-long trip to St. Louis, Missouri, along with my advisor. My trophy case was almost as impressive as my older brother's!

A Queen in the Making

Every little girl wants to wear a crown, and I was no different. The dream had been sparked when I was in the sixth grade. I looked on with admiration as Debbie Turner won the Miss America title in 1990. *What would it be like to wear a crown?* I thought. It never occurred to me that I would one day experience that wonderful feeling. I watched the pageant every year as one queen after another won the coveted title. It wasn't until the fall of 1992 that I gained the courage to fill out an application for American Coed Pageants. To my surprise, I was selected as a contestant.

In summer 1993, I completed in my first pageant. I didn't place, but was one of the twelve out of fifty contestants who made the final round. Nonetheless, the experience of being a part of such an event was success to me. I went on to compete in three more pageants while in high school, placing second in one and reaching the final round in the rest. In one pageant, I was even voted Miss Congeniality!

I found that my short pageant career gave me the opportunity to grow in several areas. I gained more of the much-needed self-esteem that had so long been missing from my life. I developed poise and self-confidence. In addition, the pageants encouraged me to develop and voice my personal and career ambitions to the world. I learned that no answer was complete without the phrase "world peace" (just a little pageant humor!).

Cindy Lumpkin

A Tribute to Parents and Teachers

I experienced a tremendous transformation during high school. Not even the negative situations could set me back. I was determined to be something bigger and better. Just when I thought things couldn't get any better, I learned that my essay had been chosen over many other honor students' papers, and I was one of two student speakers at graduation!

When I sat down to write that speech, I wanted to express gratitude to my mother, and to Mrs. Bly, Mrs. Jones, and Mrs. Tucker, those special-education teachers who worked so hard to help me learn. I knew that it was their dedication, love, and support that had enabled me to reach the point of being able to manage my disability. I was still, however, unable to admit who I was. The pain, shame, and embarrassment were too fresh for me to relive, so I expressed as much as I could without giving anything away, including not naming those who had the greatest and most positive impact on me. As my family, friends, and teachers looked on, I spoke articulately:

Good evening, Dr. Wainwright, Mr. Wright, parents, and fellow graduates. Tonight, it is most fitting that we pay special tribute to you, our parents and teachers, for your invaluable roles in helping us to be what we are today and where we are tonight.

Over the years, you have watched us grow. You taught us right from wrong, to respect ourselves, and to believe in ourselves. You were always there when we needed a helping hand or a shoulder to cry on. These are just a few of the many things you, our parents and teachers, have taught us.

We came into this world with very limited knowledge; however, you set out on the long hard task of preparing us to be able to take care of ourselves one day. You, our parents, were there, encouraging us to utter our first words. You helped us make the transition from crawling to walking. Then you set about teaching us personal hygiene.

By the age of five, you had taught us how to put on our clothes, tie our shoes, and brush our teeth. You also taught us to write our names, say our ABCs, and count; thus preparing us for our first day of school. From there, you, our teachers, imparted your knowledge to all of us. You continued to guide us through teaching and example to be the best we could be. During our thirteen years of schooling, we have had many teachers who have influenced our lives in so many ways. We will always remember you. You are the ones who helped decide what path our lives would take after tonight. This decision you helped us make will indeed affect the rest of our lives.

By dedicating your lives to educating and rearing children into young adults, you have shown our communities that you are not afraid to invest in the hopes and dreams of youth. Because of you, our dreams are coming true.

We give to you our thanks, because you have given us emotional support and encouragement, and helped us gain the confidence we needed to become the well-rounded and highly motivated individuals we are today. As parents and teachers, you can hopefully look with pride at the children you have reared and educated. We all are the products of caring people who have taught their children well.

As parents when you were teaching us to ride a bike for the first time and we fell down, you told us to get back up and try again. That was to be one of the best lessons we would learn. You knew that life would be very much like learning to ride a bike. In teaching us that lesson, you knew there would be times in our lives when we would fall down. You also knew that if we were to accomplish anything in life, we would have to learn how to get back up and keep on trying until we reached our goal. You, our teachers, also continued to reinforce this lesson daily.

If, as I stand before you this evening, you are feeling proud of my fellow classmates and me, then you should feel proud of yourselves. The way we are and hope to be has come from a solid foundation set by you, our parents and teachers. We are what we are and where we are because of you. For this, we again say thank you and we love you.

Applause erupted when I finished the speech in front of a thousand or more. I had spoken from the heart with passion and conviction. I only hoped my mother and my special-education teachers were able to hear the underlying message that I really wanted to convey. I had struggled with learning, reading, and spelling, but because of my mother and teachers, I now stood on the threshold of the rest of my life, equipped with all the necessary tools to succeed, and they had helped me acquire them.

Before continuing, I must, as an adult, a teacher, and an individual with a learning disability, explain my present-day feelings about the special-education program. I want all of you reading this, especially those who have learning disabilities, to know that the special-education program is a wonderful thing. I credit my success to the program, which has too long been considered a place to consign prospective failures. As a result of that separation, people benefiting from its services have been ostracized. The program isn't specifically designed to help students adjust to being in it, but it *is* designed to help those who qualify for its services to achieve academic success. Too often, that success is overshadowed by low self-esteem and learned helplessness. It was the latter that caused me to strive with all my might to be seen as "regular." I couldn't understand that being in special education didn't make me any less regular than anyone else. I have since grown to understand that my brain simply processes information differently, and, as a result, I learn a little differently. That's O.K.! In fact, some of the most brilliant minds and most talented people learn just like I do.

Had I understood special education as a student I would not have striven so hard to disassociate myself from it. I would still have worked hard to compete with my regular-education peers, but I would have used the program to achieve that goal. My college years would have been less stressful had I self-identified and used the services that were available to me as a person with a learning disability.

I say all this in hope that you will not let yourself be defined by your education or any label put on you. Only you can define your success and who you are. Use every resource available to achieve all you want to — including the services of the special-education program.

Redefined

Whoever said that college years are the best years of your life was not telling a lie. Becoming a student at Virginia Union University was the best decision I have made to date. At that stage of my life I slowly started to understand who I am and began coming to grips with the part of me I tried so hard to hide for so many years.

Unlike the secondary education I received in Southampton public schools, my college education was truly about self-directed development and learning. In this environment, I was encouraged to explore ideas from multiple perspectives, and formulate my own opinions, rather than just performing rote memorization and regurgitation.

BELIEF SYSTEM

At VUU I created a philosophy of life and of education. I was guided in developing this crucial viewpoint as a member of the School of Education where I became a "Reflective Explorer." I firmly believe that to succeed in education and in life requires 10 percent ability and 90 percent attitude. Your attitude is your greatest resource. It directs all that will be in your life.

While a student at Virginia Union and as a result of my education there, I started to mourn for the child who endured shame and ridicule as a result of a label. The pain of shame, doubt, frustration, and confusion were unnecessary. My education enabled me to realize that my issues with school could have been solved with a different approach to teaching and learning. The solution had been around for years. In fact, studying the great educational theorists of the past is the foundation for most successful post-secondary teacher training programs.

Early on in my training to become an educator, I made the observation that not all children will be "A" students, no matter how hard they try. Our society places too much emphasis on grades and test scores, and not enough on learning. We must learn to encourage the learning ability of all students, no matter their level of performance. Therefore, just as Jean Paige's theory suggests, teachers should recognize the abilities and limits of students at each level of cognitive development and provide appropriate learning activities. Children should be encouraged to develop the skills and mental operations relevant to their mental stage, and should be prepared to grow toward the next stage. Teachers, from early childhood through secondary school, need to develop appropriate educational environments and work with students individually according to each one's level of readiness. Had this been a practice while I was a young student, I am certain that none of the students who shared my special-education class would have had to deal with the negative side of having been labeled LD.

Over the course of my stay at VUU my professors guided me in "developing and refining the characteristics of the Reflective Explorer — having competence, having an ethic of caring, using an adaptive approach to constructivist teaching [and learning], and being a skillful manager"

"Reflective inquiry is the central structure of each of these components and the process for which candidates [in the teacher education program at VUU] prepare and evaluate learning" (VUU).

CONVICTED

It was this process that inspired a need to analyze my past, present, and future, using variations of the four components of the reflector explorer to elevate me to a higher understanding of self.

From the first day I set foot on the campus of Virginia Union University, the administration, faculty, and staff were telling us students how great we were. "It's no accident that you are here," they would say. "You are the leaders of tomorrow, and these hallowed grounds and dear old walls are your training ground. Union has a rich history of cultivating the minds of some of our nation's greatest leaders."

They never let us forget it. Armed with this new information, the past became a blur in my memory — until my second year in college, that is. I was sitting in my Introduction to Education class, praying that the professor wouldn't call on me to read the article that lay before me, an article about Ennis Cosby, written at the time of his death. My prayer was answered; someone else read it. "Thank you, God!"

The article explained his difficulties in school, and his eventual discovery that they were due to a learning disability. As my classmate read the details, my eyes filled with tears. I tried to blink them away, but they kept coming. His life seemed a replica of my own, but there was a major difference: upon learning of his disability, Ennis Cosby devoted his life to helping others who struggled with the same problem; I, on the other hand, spent mine trying to forget and imagining that I wasn't learning-disability gifted.

At that moment, I became a reflective explorer in the rough. For what seemed like hours but was only minutes, I finally allowed myself to reflect on and evaluate my educational history.

I had spent most of my energy distancing myself from the special-education program, both physically and mentally. I had packed away all the embarrassment I suffered while in the program, and convinced myself that it never existed. I tried to live my life as if I was a "normal" student. Instead of using my education for personal empowerment, I let my grades define who I was. I failed to realize that no matter what grades I made, the fact that I am an individual with a learning disability would never change. I finally admitted to myself who I am, and understood my purpose in life. I realized that I am a person with a learning disability who has been given the opportunity to serve as a teacher and role model for both the disabled and non-disabled.

My learning disability is something I will never outgrow, despite having been blessed with a couple of good teachers who helped me find ways to compensate for my shortcomings. I had wonderful role models, and perhaps most important, I had a loving, supportive mother who loved me unconditionally, and I had somehow developed the skills and determination necessary to set and achieve goals.

The very next day I changed my major to Exceptional Education.

A New Path

It amazed me how much I was able to connect my past scholastic experiences to my learning as an Exceptional Education major. I often amazed my professor and classmates with my knowledge of special education. The professor would ask questions that no one else was able to answer. He was baffled by how quickly I was able to retain information. Neither my professors nor my classmates had any idea that I was referring to and building upon prior knowledge; that I was already an expert in the field, having experienced firsthand what they had only read about or observed in others.

Although I already knew plenty about special education, I learned a lot more. For example, I had never given a thought to the actual nature of my disability, and hadn't realized that there were categories. I thought I was just– well– you know… retarded. Even when I realized that was not so, I still didn't know what I was.

In the special-education program, no distinctions had ever been made among us; we were just lumped together. Until my sophomore year at VUU, I didn't know why I'd been a special-education student. I had always wanted to believe that I'd been mislabeled. Because of my change of major, however, I learned that exceptionality comes in many different types.

Of course, with knowledge comes awareness. My curiosity was piqued. I wanted to confirm that I had been called SLD (specific learning disability). There was only one problem: I was afraid of what I might discover. I knew the characteristics I had displayed as a child, many of them typical of people with learning disabilities, but I wondered whether the label I was given matched the traits I displayed.

I mustered up the courage to ask a middle school special-education teacher with whom I had maintained contact. She said, "Well, you really can't be anything other than LD." I felt a little silly for feeling the need to have someone else confirm something I should have known, but her statement enabled me to breath a sigh of relief.

The most pertinent information I gathered in my first special-education course at VUU was the definition of "learning disability." It means "a disorder in one or more of the basic psychological processes involved in understanding or using language, spoken or written, which may manifest in an imperfect ability to listen, think, speak, read, write, spell, or do mathematical calculations." The term is generically applied to many different disabling conditions. Most important however, it's not an intellectual disability, meaning that it doesn't necessarily affect an individual's level of intelligence.

In recent years, it has been estimated that there are 30 million people in the United States with LD, the vast majority of them with average or above-average IQs. In fact, some of the world's smartest and most talented people have learning disabilities.

Knowing this as a youngster could have made a world of difference. Like so many other students, I struggled with the issue of identity. Perhaps some of the derogatory words associated with the special-education program, such as "dungeon" and "slow," would not have hurt so much; perhaps I would have realized that being LD gifted was not a death sentence. Maybe I wouldn't have put so much energy into hating who I was and trying to be someone I'm not.

***

On May 1991, while in seventh grade, three years after my initial evaluation for the special-education program, I underwent my first re-evaluation. I was actually excited about the test this time, knowing the stakes involved — an opportunity to test out of the program. Before we were halfway through the testing, I lost all hope of ever being a "regular" student. I sat across from the psychologist, who called out words that I had no ideal how to spell. Despite a tremendous effort to spell the words phonetically, the sounds meant little to me; they just didn't make much sense. The more I sounded them out, the more defeated I felt. Eventually, I gave up on getting the spelling even remotely correct. I recall feeling uncertain about every word I wrote that day.

The test devastated me. Perhaps, however, it wouldn't have had the same effect had I known there was a reason why I couldn't spell those words. I thought it was because I was unintelligent. Predictably, I was found eligible for continued services.

***

Changing my major had been good for me. Eventually, in my studies at Virginia Union, I found the answers to my questions. Although they were textbook answers, I understood why I'd been labeled LD despite the ability to compete academically, often taking advanced classes, with regular-education students. I knew why I, an honor student at the top of her class, still suffered anxiety attacks at the thought of being called upon to read aloud in class, and why I had difficulty spelling words that I should have known how to spell. The answers weren't enough to make me go public with my learning disability — at least not yet. I convinced myself that it was sufficient that someday I would forever change the lives of students with disabilities.

It wasn't until summer 2001 that I decided to share my story by writing this book. I had envisioned the process in 1998, but upon awakening the next day, the idea seemed less vivid than it had the night before. I told myself that I had let my imagination run away with me again, there was no way I was capable of writing a book, and I pushed the idea aside.

Praise to the Women on My Journey

To the women on my journey
Who showed me the ways to go and ways not to go,
Whose strength and compassion held up a torch of light
and beckoned me to follow,
Whose weakness and ignorance darkened the path and
encouraged me to turn another way.
To the women on my journey
Who showed me how to live and how not to live,
Whose grace, success and gratitude lifted me into the
fullness of surrender to God,
Whose bitterness, envy and wasted gifts warned me
away from the emptiness of self-will.
To the women on my journey

Who showed me what I am and what I am not,
Whose love, encouragement and confidence held me tenderly and nudged me gently,
Whose judgment, disappointment and lack of faith called me to deeper levels of commitment and resolve.
To the women on my journey who taught me love by means of both darkness and light,
To these women I say bless you and thank you from the depths of my heart, for I have been healed and set free through your joy and through your sacrifice.

— Rev. Melissa M. Bowers

Many men and women have influenced my life, some with greater impact than others. I believe that we can take something positive from any negative situation we encounter. Everyone who impacted me has changed my life for the better, whether I viewed our interaction as positive or negative.

I believe that people are placed in our path for a reason. Sometimes we know the reason instantly, or we learn it a bit later, or we might never know why we crossed paths with another person, but if we examine our experiences, we can take something beneficial from each of them.

For a time, I was bitter about various encounters I'd had with teachers who weren't knowledgeable about educating students with disabilities or who were generally insensitive to my plight. Some damaged me in ways that are difficult to express, and others left scars that I'm still trying to heal. Nonetheless, I can see the positive in many of these experiences. They taught me what I *don't* want to be.

Moses Norman, one of my professors at Clark Atlanta University, once said, "The mark of an excellent teacher is a teacher who will teach differently from what he/she was taught." Had I not encountered teachers like Mrs. Trigg, Mrs. Ward, and Mrs. Baskin, I would never have known how *not* to teach. Because of them, I am a teacher full of compassion and love; I am an encourager and confidence builder, and all that they weren't for me. Their "ignorance darkened the path and encouraged me to turn another way."

Just as some individuals showed me the ways not to go, there were others "whose strength and compassion held up a torch of light and beckoned me to follow." They were my saving grace, and I will forever be indebted to their caring spirits.

Praise to Tamara Wellons

Tamara was the first woman I would meet on my educational journey. At the time she was more a mature young adult than a woman. Though we were the same age, I was in the sixth grade and she was in the seventh. Compared to all the other seventh graders, both male and female, Tamara stood out.

She had such charisma and leadership ability that it was hard to believe she was only twelve years old. She sang, played an instrument in the school band, and became president of the Student Government Association in her eighth grade year.

I admired her ever since becoming a student at Southampton Middle School, but it was a short conversation we had at the end of her eighth grade year that won her a place in my heart forever and encouraged me to become a leader.

I was going to class one day, walking very slowly to keep anyone from seeing me enter the dungeon, when Tamara stopped me. She said, "Cindy, have you thought about running for president of the Student Government Association next year?"

I must have looked at her like she was crazy. She went on to say, "I believe you would do a good job." I couldn't believe this conversation was taking place — the most popular girl at my school, whom I greatly admired, was suggesting that I take over her position as SGA president! Unsure that I was capable, I told her I would think about running for vice president. She said again that I should run for president, and ended the conversation by telling me to think about it.

Running for president never entered my mind, even after our conversation, but the fact that Tamara Wellons told me she thought I would make a good president was all that mattered at that point. Eventually, I did run, and won the position of vice president.

Though Tamara and I never became friends, we remained associates; I respected her as if she were my best friend, and have never lost that respect for her. I supported her with my vote in every election she took part in during high school.

After graduation I never saw Tamara again, but a mutual friend updated me from time to time. During my reign as Miss Virginia Union University, that friend told me that Tamara had been Miss Bowie State University 1998–99 the year before and was now an educator. I never imagined that I would one day see myself just as I saw the charming twelve-year-old young adult, Tamara Wellons.

Praise to "Bug"

Bug was my hair stylist and my first adult friend. I admired her from the first day I walked into the hair salon, because she struck me as a very sincere, generous person, and I respected her as I would a best friend. Bug talked to me just as she did her older customers. She would ask about school and the sports I played and my opinion on certain topics.

After a time, we developed a relationship in which she was comfortable revealing personal information about her life. She talked about her college experience and her family. She shared with me what I know had to be painful memories of a failed marriage and the reasons for its demise.

Our relationship was definitely not a typical friendship. We saw one another once or twice a month. The stories she shared were usually about people in our community. I saw Bug as a strong black woman doing what was necessary to raise her family while capturing some happiness for herself. At an early age she had made the hard decision to chart her own course in life rather than follow anyone else's. I admired her strength and courage, and valued her friendship. Bug never treated me like a child, or like someone whom she thought lacked intelligence. On those visits to the hair salon, I felt- well… normal — which was great.

Praise to Coach Jones and Jackie Corker

On the day I moved into the dormitory at Virginia Union University, I was reintroduced to Jackie Corker. A longtime family friend, Jackie had seen my mother leaving the campus after helping me get settled. Jackie quickly inquired about my presence, and my mother informed her that I was now a student there. Jackie, who had known me when I was a child, came to my room. From there, our friendship blossomed.

Stacey Jones was my college volleyball coach. Our paths crossed during my sophomore year. Coach, as she was often called, was the epitome of grace, beauty, style, and intelligence. She was an excellent role model for my teammates and me, and, as it happened, she and I had a lot in common.

At that time, both women were dealing with troubles of their own. Jackie was married and had a small child, and Stacey was just establishing herself in her profession. Still, they found the time to guide me through those transitional years at the university; I could count on them for anything.

One day I emailed Stacey to tell her that I was in the process of writing a book. She emailed back, "Make sure you get a good editor." I thought the statement hilarious. She didn't know about my disability at the time. When we were at Virginia Union, *she* was my editor. In fact, she critiqued all the speeches and correspondence for my role as Miss Virginia Union University. More than once, I vowed not to let her read my work anymore because I felt embarrassed when she found errors that I should have been able to identify. Whenever I heard "God, girl!" I knew she'd found something. Stacey must have thought it odd to read the work of a college student with a GPA of 3.7 and find the errors that she found, but she never looked down on me. I was grateful for that. When she reads this book, I'm sure my confession won't surprise her. It will explain a lot — after all, Stacey is a special-education teacher.

It would take an entire book to adequately describe my relationships with Jackie and Stacey, so I won't attempt it. I will say, however, that had I not met these women, my life would have been entirely different. Jackie and Stacy were my angels, sent during the college years to help prepare me for the next stage in life. I am forever indebted to them for their sincerity, generosity, and friendship.

Praise to Josephine Barksdale

Mrs. Barksdale and I crossed paths on Sept. 7, 2001, a meeting truly arrange by God. After being in Atlanta for one year and needing only two classes to complete my master's degree in Educational Leadership and Administration, I decided it was time to start a teaching career. Because I wasn't financially stable, that desire had to be placed on hold, and I was forced to accept a live-in position as a residence director on the campus of Clark Atlanta University. The public school year had begun as I underwent the three-week training period for the position. I needed a place to live, and was unable to be in both places at once, so teaching would have to wait until the following year.

Soon after the school year began at Clark Atlanta, I received a letter from the Atlanta Public School System stating that there were still teaching vacancies. Interested, I called to inquire into the available positions and was given a list of schools to contact. I received the same reply from each prospective employer: "We filled our last position only days ago." Finally, someone said, "Let me have someone get back to you."

I received a phone call from Mrs. Barksdale the very next day, and an interview was scheduled for the following day, September 7, 2001. In the interview, Mrs. Barksdale described how she ran her department. I was impressed with the way she operated. Mrs. Barksdale explained the various partnerships that were set up to help special-education students make the transition from school to work or from school to school. I thought this was amazing.

This special-education program was far more advanced than at other schools where I'd had the opportunity to observe. Too often, these programs are established for compliance purposes — if they are established at all. This was different; there was something special about Mrs. Barksdale. I knew I wanted to work with her and learn from her.

At the end of the interview, Mrs. Barksdale stood up, shook my hand, and thanked me for coming. It was her next words that reached me in a way that I had never before been touched. "By the way, I am LD gifted," she said. I was stunned; for a while I just stared at her, unable to speak. Had I heard her incorrectly? To make sure, I said, "You are!" After blinking back the tears that had instantly formed, I said, "I am as well."

Mrs. Barksdale was the first person to whom I ever admitted my secret. Moreover, she was the first and the only person I knew who had a learning disability and was living a productive, successful professional life. A great weight was lifted off my shoulders. It felt good to admit it without feeling embarrassed and stupid. More importantly, my encounter with Mrs. Barksdale validated my hopes and dreams for the future — if she was able to make it, then so could I!

The Need for Heroes

Tamara, Bug, Stacey, Jackie, and Mrs. Barksdale are all individuals whom I continue to admire. They showed me what was possible, and inspired me to be the best I could be. They helped me along the path, and will forever remain in my heart. They are my heroes, and I will always see them as my "lifelines," but as I learn and grow, I need to find new lifelines; to continue seeking out people who will inspire me to reach further milestones. By having lifelines, we tap into a tremendous source of renewed strength and belief that we can do anything. Our lifelines not only inspire us, but also make things look easy. That's what moves us to want to be just like them and better: "If they can do it, so can I"

Part II

A Journey into Your Past, Present and Future

The Individual as Reflective Explorer

The term "Reflective Explorer" is used in conjunction with the conceptual framework of the Department of Education at Virginia Union University. The university seeks to guide students in developing the ideal characteristics of good teachers:

- competence;
- an ethic of caring;
- an adaptive approach to constructivist teaching;
- the ability to manage skillfully.

During my studies at Virginia Union, the term took on a double meaning. The traits of the reflective explorer not only helped me to become the ideal teacher candidate, but also served as tools for redefining who I was. By reshaping the conceptual framework of the education department, I custom-designed it to fit me. The process was not difficult, as I had already been given an excellent model. I simply applied the components to my life instead of looking at them from an academic viewpoint, realizing that I had to use these components to improve my own life before I could use them to better the lives of my future students. I had to learn how to love myself as well as others, even those who might not always have my best interest in mind. I had to learn how to take different approaches with people, especially with my learning. I had to learn to extract the positive from every situation and emerge from each experience with a lesson learned. Finally, I had to learn how to manage my life in a way that would make me happy and that would be beneficial to society. This was how I coined the phrase "The Individual as Reflective Explorer."

The individual as reflective explorer is simply one who has developed the characteristics of self-competence, skillful management, and the ethic of caring, and operates with a constructivist perspective, in order to learn the lessons of the past and use the present as a guide for shaping the future.

The Individual as Reflective Explorer

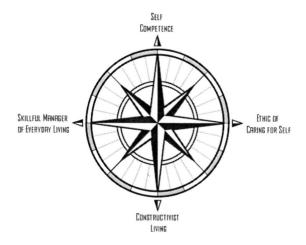

Self-competence

Self-competence is expert understanding of your life. It entails thorough knowledge of your past, accurate perception of your present emotional, physical, and spiritual state, and knowing what you want out of life. It also involves having a well-thought-out plan of action for reaching your goals. When you know yourself, you know what you're capable of accomplishing; you know your competency level.

ETHIC OF CARING FOR SELF

Ethic of caring for self is not only valuing oneself, but valuing all of humankind. Caring for self, said Thomas Merton, is "desiring to live, accepting life as a very great gift and great good, not because of what it gives you, but because of what it enables you to give others." Simply stated, it is caring enough to give yourself the best, which allows you to give your best to all.

SKILLFUL MANAGER OF EVERYDAY LIVING

The skillful manager is the individual who systematically organizes day-to-day living so as to produce a desired outcome in the future.

CONSTRUCTIVIST LIVING

The constructivist is able to adapt to change in everyday living, while living life to the fullest. No matter what circumstances arise, the constructivist has the ability to face them head-on, confident of overcoming. Constructivist living is simply the ability to change as necessary to survive and thrive in the current environment.

The point of becoming a reflective explorer is to grow into a self-actualized individual (one who has a thorough knowledge of self). Many psychologists believe that becoming self-actualized is a lifelong process. To an extent, I agree, but I believe that we have innate characteristics, which we display from birth to death, and it needn't take us a lifetime to figure out that we have them.

I believe that by a certain time in young people's lives they have some idea of who they are. Too often, however, young people choose to ignore who God created them to be, and reinvent themselves to be someone they see as better or more desirable.

A key reason for my success as a young student is that I was sensitive to the innate characteristics I possessed. I had no idea that, through my work ethic, I was putting the principle of determination into practice. It never occurred to me to reinvent myself as someone I deemed better than who I already was. I did, however, decide to use the qualities I deemed best in others to reinvent a better me. I never realized how powerful I was then; it wasn't until my time at Virginia Union University that I began to discover the seeds of greatness that lay within me.

My education at VUU had enormous impact on my life. The components of the Department of Education's conceptual framework guide both my professional and personal life to this day. Becoming a reflective explorer didn't happen overnight, and at every turn I had to struggle with some part of me before completing the process.

In the beginning, I refused to reflect on my educational past, because it was a past that brought only pain and shame. I didn't understand the benefits of coming to terms with the fact that I have a learning disability. Although I had successfully assimilated into regular education, and considered this a great success, it was the use of the conceptual framework that enabled me to analyze the past and answer questions about my past, present, and future.

Despite my internal issues with the past, the framework guided me in learning about who I was. I discovered non-academic reasons for the circumstances that perplexed me the longest. For example, why did my life turn out so differently from the lives of those who shared the dungeon with me?

When I was in the seventh grade and being served in the special-education program, my classmate Sue and I would challenge one another on class work and exams. We pushed each other to earn the highest grades in our class. Often, I lost out to Sue, but somewhere down the line her fire seemed to go out. Like so many others who shared the dungeon with us, she gave up. Tired of fighting, she accepted what was given and no longer pushed herself to higher achievement. My academic ability was no greater or smaller than Sue's; she had simply lost her drive. Like most people, including myself at one point, she began to wander through life unconsciously, unaware of the greatness she possessed. She did not develop a sense of self — the most important knowledge anyone can acquire.

To know oneself is the alpha and the omega — the beginning and the end — of living a life of harmony, dreaming and implementing the steps necessary to make your dreams reality. Self-knowledge is personal empowerment. Instead, Sue let her circumstances and mental conditioning define who she was and then lived her life accordingly.

We all have circumstances that are sometimes beyond our control and that can alter our lives if we allow them to. Most people deal with their circumstances by concentrating on the negatives and totally disregarding the positives. This can lead to self-destruction.

Ponder this: Circumstance is simply a fact or event that must be considered along with other facts or events. If you disregard the positive circumstances of your life, then all you can see are the negatives. It's just like weighing out strengths and weaknesses: you have to consider both in order to have a balanced perspective on life.

For example, a boy is reared in a single-parent household. His father is considered a "deadbeat dad." By the time this boy reaches high school, he is involved in all types of illegal activities. Eventually, he is arrested and sent to jail. His sentence includes counseling, where it's discovered that this young man blames his behavior on the fact that his father is not around. When asked about his mother, the young man says that she was a great mother who taught him right from wrong.

It seems that this youngster focused on the fact that he had no father, and neglected to consider the fact that he had a terrific mother. Granted, the boy had no control over being reared without a father figure; however, he had control of how he allowed it to affect his life.

Even though our circumstances may often be beyond our control, we have the power to control their effects on our quality of life. Some people are raised in single-parent households, while others have the good fortune to be raised in two-parent homes. Some people are born into poverty, while others are born into wealth; some people are born with illnesses, while others are born healthy. Some, like me, are born with learning disabilities, while others are born without any.

All of these are circumstances that are beyond our control; circumstances that may have a tremendous impact on our lives. The key to dealing with them lies in how we respond. Millions of people have less than ideal circumstances. The question is whether you allow these circumstances to dictate how you live.

Our mental conditioning, the way we think, determines how we deal with the situations that arise. Society dictates our mental conditioning, and society fails to consider people as individuals. We are individuals first, with individual learning styles, thought processes, likes, and dislikes. We cannot be lumped into one category. Because of society's attempt to fit all of us into one category, millions of people have distorted self-concepts, because they have allowed society to dictate how they view themselves.

Society says that people who are raised in single-parent homes are more likely to experience less healthy lives, on average, than children from intact families. Statistics say that children growing up with only one parent are more likely to drop out of school, bear children out of wedlock, and have trouble keeping jobs as young adults. Society also labels people who are born into poverty as unlikely to rise above that standard of living as adults. Children of teen mothers are more likely to do poorly in school, more likely to drop out of school, and less likely to attend college. Girls born to teen mothers are themselves 22 percent more likely to become mothers as teens, and sons of teen mothers are more likely to end up in jail. Do these statistical tendencies materialize for every person who experiences the conditions that may engender them? No! The people who rise above these circumstances reject society's labels, while those who do not are most likely to accept their fates. It is mental conditioning that allows society to dictate how we respond to our circumstances. Know that circumstances can be overcome. All it takes is a change in the way you think.

As a student at Virginia Union University, I had the honor of becoming a distinguished lady of Delta Sigma Theta Sorority, Incorporated. During spring 1999, thirty-seven other young ladies joined me in becoming members of this dynamic sisterhood. Number eleven on my line, which would later be known as Another Bad Creation (ABC), was a young lady named Sharnte Wise. The circumstances of her life paralleled what happens to many women today: Sharnte became a teenage mother. Some of her family and friends shunned her, and her education became an uphill battle, one that this courageous young lady faced head-on.

While completing high school, Sharnte raised her daughter with minimal family support. She knew that if she wanted to give her child a good life, she would have to continue her education. She decided to become a full-time student and mother. Balancing her education, parent-teacher conferences, and her daughter's education was not easy. Sharnte had to make sacrifices, and wasn't always able to enjoy the life of a carefree college student. The fact that her fiancé was serving in the armed forces abroad didn't make matters any better. Nonetheless, Sharnte pressed on and, six years after becoming a student at Virginia Union University, she graduated with a bachelor's degree in accounting.

Now married to her child's father, working for a prestigious law firm, and raising a respectful, well disciplined, and intelligent ten-year-old daughter, Sharnte did not allow her circumstances to hold her back from reaching her goals. She refused to become the statistic that society said she would probably become as a result of her teen pregnancy.

As George Bernard Shaw said, "The people who get on in this world are the people who get up and look for the circumstances they want, and, if they can't find them, they make them." Sharnte Wise did just that. She created the circumstances she wanted, and her life is better for it.

When one door is closed to us, we must find another that is open. I emerged from my undergraduate experience believing that I could achieve anything. Thus when the College of William & Mary rejected my application to become a graduate student there, my bubble burst. A door to my education had been closed. When Clark Atlanta University wrote me saying, "...you have been admitted to the School of Education to pursue a Master of Arts degree in the Department of Educational Leadership" another door had been opened.

On May 20, 2002, I graduated with a 4.0 grade point average and a master's degree from the only HBCU (Historically Black College or University) listed in *U.S. News and World Report*'s Best Colleges, 2000. I found the circumstances that I wanted at Clark Atlanta University.

I believe wholeheartedly that once you have developed a heightened sense of self, you start to deviate from the norm. You no longer try to fill other people's shoes, but instead forge your own way. You create your own definitions of life, happiness, intelligence, success, and failure. Becoming a reflective explorer of self helped me achieve this finely tuned sense of self, and it helped Sharnte Wise defy the odds against a teenage mother becoming successful.

As a reflective explorer, I am charting my course through life at my own pace and defining success for myself. This involves the process of first becoming an expert at knowing myself, my uniqueness, the special gifts and qualities that make me who I am. As you begin your journey toward becoming a reflective explorer, I encourage you to open yourself to the idea of truly getting to know you. Don't be afraid to be who you are and understand that you alone have complete control of your destiny.

Allow my story of becoming a reflective explorer to inspire you to take the journey yourself. No matter what your circumstances, this process will benefit you. To live a happy life that includes achieving our goals, we must become in tune with who we are. We must understand how our experiences have shaped who we are and formed our emotional state. Are you ready for the journey of a lifetime? Let's go!

There is Healing in the Past

What do I mean by loving ourselves properly? I mean, first of all, desiring to live, accepting life as a very great gift and a great good, not because of what it gives us, but because of what it enables us to give others.

— Thomas Merton

Writing this book became my avenue for making peace with my past, a past that wreaked havoc with my self-esteem, and drove me to strive with all my power to reach a goal that seemed unattainable.

I tried to define myself by being in regular-education classes and making good grades. I thought that would make me "regular." Somewhere along the way, I conceived the notion that I was bad, stupid, and crazy because I had a learning disability. I didn't realize that all the A's I made would never erase the fact of my learning disability. I have succeeded in many ways. I have overcome seemingly insurmountable obstacles, and learned to compensate for my disability, but that success came at a price I should not have had to pay. I lost the part that makes me special and unique — my sense of self.

On my journey of personal growth, I realized that I tried to hide the fact that I have a learning disability instead of embracing it. I no longer do that. It's time for me to celebrate who I am. I hope that you'll begin to celebrate who you are and who you will become on the path to realizing your hopes and dreams. Stand up and be proud of who you are. Take control of your circumstances, life, and destiny. If I could do it, then so can you!

While writing this book, I was able to regain that part of me I lost so long ago. I was able to go back in time to deal with my past, put it into proper perspective, and make peace with it. No one is able to change the past, but we can most certainly come to grips with it and change the course of our future.

Cindy Lumpkin

BECOMING A REFLECTIVE EXPLORER

No one ever emerges from their past unaffected. No one else can claim to know who you are, your fears, your victories, your defeats, and your pains. No one but you truly knows your plight in this life — not your parents, foes, friends, preachers, or teachers.

Journeying into my past was difficult, but was ultimately a liberating experience. There are many avenues you can take to bridge the gap between your past, present, and future. The most effective tool for me thus far has been this personal narrative. I not only recollected my past, but also gathered all the information at my disposal: old pictures, yearbooks, school records, test scores, and even friends and teachers.

During that expedition, I discovered some very intriguing facts that I hadn't previously been aware of or understood. To my disappointment, when I went to retrieve my school file, it had been purged of all information pertaining to the evaluation of my eligibility for the special-education program. The only remaining record of the program was the front page of an IEP from the ninth grade, confirming that I was categorized as LD, which gave me a sense of closure.

The file did contain important standardized test scores. During our junior year, all eleventh graders were given the Test of Achievement and Proficiency. On the complete composite, which is an average of scores on reading comprehension, mathematics, and written expression, using sources of information, social studies, and science tests, I scored in the fifty-seventh percentile. This means that I scored better than 57 percent of the eleventh grade students nationally who took the test, and 43 percent scored as well as or better than I did. When broken down into categories, I scored in the seventy-fifth percentile in science, the sixty-seventh percentile in social studies, and the sixtieth percentile in written expression.

What makes these results so compelling for me is that for so long I thought I was unintelligent, but those scores don't reflect lack of intelligence. Despite having felt academically inadequate for most of my life, my standardized test score doesn't justify such feelings. In science, I did better then 75 percent of all the students who took the test. I scored well on the written expression portion, too, an area in which I feel my disability affects me more deeply.

What did the expedition into school records show me? First, what I thought was my weakest area turned out to be one of my strongest. Above all else, it showed me that I am not stupid. Seeing is believing, and reading these scores and connecting them with my knowledge of the characteristics of persons with learning disabilities gave me great clarity about my situation.

When most people think of anyone in a special-education program, they immediately envision someone who is incapable of learning or who has a below-average IQ. I was once guilty of this, and I encounter educators daily who have low expectations of students who qualify for special-education services. It's difficult for many to believe that a highly intelligent person is unable to do some of the things that are the supposed marks of intelligence.

Can one be intelligent and yet be unable to read, spell, write, or do math? There are millions of people who, despite the fact that they may not be capable of reading, spelling, or mathematics, are exceptionally intelligent.

Exploring my past helped me understand that intelligence is not the sum of how well one reads, writes, spells, and does math. It was hard to take this journey because I was afraid of what I might find, but it was essential in order to become a true reflective explorer. Sometimes we are so busy living in the moment that we are blind to what our circumstances actually are. That's why it's so important to visit your past and find the keys to why you are where you are now. Because you are no longer living the past, it makes it much easier to see things clearly.

Have you ever said or done something and then, moments later, realized, "I shouldn't have done that?" Most of us have. Even though we couldn't go back and undo what we did, or say the things we wish we had, we used our new knowledge to guide our future decision making. If you know and understand your past, you can construct a bright future for yourself. As you begin your journey to becoming a reflective explorer, keep these things in mind:

1. Be compassionate;
2. Identify the major events;

3. Identify your wounds;
4. Identify your victories;
5 Identify your lifelines;
6. Identify lessons learned.

Step 1. Have compassion for all the major players in your life, the people whose words and actions left a lasting impression upon you. It's crucial to learn to forgive them and show compassion for the wrongs they may have done. Developmental psychologist Robert Enright defines forgiveness as giving up the resentment to which you are entitled, and offering the person(s) who hurt you friendlier attitudes to which they are not entitled. By deciding to forgive, you start the process of healing yourself. You can't start this healing until you begin to forgive, because people who refuse to forgive remain in the power of whoever injured them. When you allow yourself to stay angry with people, you give them control over your life and allow them to limit the progress you make in your emotional, spiritual, and physical development. You allow them to rob you of achieving your goals. Forgiveness is essential for your continued growth and maturation.

Your ability to forgive can happen quickly or it might take years. Enright believes that there is a step-by-step process to forgiving others, which includes:

- facing up to the anger, shame, or hurt;
- recognizing the source of the hurt;

- choosing to forgive;
- finding a new way to think about the person who wronged you; and
- trying on the shoes of the other person.

Looking back on my anger, I realize that it took me a long time to forgive. I denied that I was angry because I refused to face the fact that I was a special-education student with a disability. I made myself believe that I had been mislabeled. My life and my learning did not improve until I was able to recognize what was causing me to be so angry. I was upset at being unable to read and spell as well as my contemporaries could. I resented being in special-education classes. After I started looking at my life and learning more realistically, however, I was able to improve my reading and spelling. Often, I had to go the extra mile; I had to study more, but after I began seeing the results, the extra hours didn't seem to matter. The important thing was that I was able to read and learn just like anyone else.

That was just the beginning of my forgiveness process. Next, I had to make a conscious decision about whether to try to forgive all those teachers whose low expectations and whose behavior toward me helped foster my feelings of low self-worth. I chose to forgive, deciding to give those wrongdoers the benefit of the doubt. Perhaps they really didn't understand how their words and actions affected me. As a first-year teacher, my healing process had come full circle. I was able to put myself in those teachers' shoes. I had never understood how stressful teaching can be. This is no excuse for treating students poorly, but stress and pressure can have a great effect on our judgment.

I realize now that I went through Enright's forgiveness process unknowingly. Eventually, my feelings and attitude started to change, and I began to experience true compassion for my offenders. I finally understood what was meant by "Compassion is the ultimate and most meaningful embodiment of emotional maturity." Many people believe that it is through compassion that we achieve the highest peak in our search for self-fulfillment. Once I had developed compassion and had forgiven, my anxiety and depression diminished and hope and self-esteem increased.

As you revisit your past, try not to blame your players or be angry about the things they may have done or didn't do. This emotional journey is about forgiveness and understanding.

Step 2. Identify the major events in your life. Try to pin point those milestone occurrences that caused you pain and that still burn brightly in your memory. Analyze each as if it were a puzzle piece; try to understand why it stayed with you and why it is so important. No event is too small — if it altered your life in any way, then it's worth reliving. This process may be painful, but there is power in knowing your past. If you learn from that knowledge, it will ultimately help you direct your future in a positive way.

You might want to try to give meaning to your feelings by sharing them with a friend, parent, teacher, counselor, or even your classmates. You might find that their experiences are not so different from your own. In addition, you might find writing down your feelings, or making audio or video recordings, to be a healing experience. This process will give you something concrete to visit as often as you need to.

Step 3. Identify your wounds. This could be the hardest part of becoming a reflective explorer; nonetheless, you need to identify any scars left by past hurts and disappointments. Think about the times when you felt stupid or crazy or just not part of the group. Think about the events in your life that caused you great pain. Who caused you this pain? How did you react to it? Did you in turn harm others? Do you still blame and hate them because you were made to endure such treatment? As a result, have you hardened your heart against society? Do you blame someone or something for what you are or aren't? Who did you want to be? Who do you feel you are supposed to be?

Please remember that you have the power to forgive, change your mindset, and walk in compassion for any child or adult who has suffered or is suffering these same injuries.

Step 4. Identify your victories. We have all had victories and special achievements. What are yours? There are no wrong answers here, so don't hold back. What have you accomplished? What are you most proud of? Did you make the football or volleyball team? What about your impressive collection of CDs? That new job you just got is another victory. If nothing else, you awoke this morning able to see another day, and you are reading this book!

Once you start claiming your victories, it will become easier for you to identify them in the future. Being able to recognize your victories is vital, because it provides you with information that you can use to gauge your current level of progress. In addition, it's the perfect motivation. Achievement is like anything else in life: it requires you to put forth effort. Motivation gives you that extra push. Without motivation, people wander through life, doing the same old things day after day, and never progressing toward their goals.

Step 5. Identify your lifelines. In the popular TV game show *Who Wants to Be a Millionaire,* contestants are challenged with a series of questions. The more questions a contestant can answer correctly, the more money he or she wins. During the course of the game, each contestant is allowed to contact three "lifelines" — people who help answer difficult questions.

We can compare the people who help us lead more successful, fulfilling lives to those TV lifelines. These are the beautiful people who believe in us, love us, and encourage us to go on when we feel ready to give up. They see the best in us when we are unable to; they make us feel special, and are always there when we need a helping hand or a shoulder to cry on. Our lifelines can be anyone: preachers, teachers, coaches, parents, siblings, friends, hairdressers, or strangers — anyone who cheers us on as we race toward fulfilling our goals. We may have known some of our lifelines for a very long time, while we've crossed paths with others for only for a brief moment. Nonetheless, these people have touched our lives in a most profound way. I encourage you to start thinking about your lifelines. In what ways have they been there for you? What might you and your situation be had they not been there?

Step 6. Identify lessons learned. So far, you've answered some key questions about yourself, but there's an even greater question to answer. What have you learned from your experiences? Have you hardened your heart against society's ignorance? Have you learned to treat others as you were treated? Are you more objective rather than subjective?

As I said earlier, no one escapes the past unaffected. Some of our experiences have a very evident positive impact on our lives; others less so. Still, all our past experiences, good and bad, are ultimately positive.

Do you remember when you learned the meaning of the word "hot" by touching a stove or an iron? The experience wasn't pleasant, was it? Still, the pain of touching that hot object taught you not to touch it again. Few people would consider burning themselves a positive experience. Looking at it from the perspective of having learned a lesson, though, you just might view it as having been positive. You learned that touching something hot will burn you. Because you learned, the painful act of getting burned led to a positive outcome — it prevented you from getting burned again. No matter what situations arise, no matter what you've gone through or are going through now, you can learn from it, grow, and become a better person as a result.

Life is a ball of physical and mental experience. The more you experience, the more you learn, and the wiser you become. The wiser you are, the better decisions you make. Since your decisions guide and shape your life, when you make wise choices, your life will be better, and you'll be happier. In the end, the key to a happy, successful life is your ability to learn from experience. If you can't, then you won't experience the fullness of life from childhood to death. Learning and growing through that progression is what makes life worth living.

ACTION PLANNER

Developing an Ethic of Caring for Self

The ethic of caring for self is not only having a value of love for oneself, but also for all of humanity. Caring for self is caring enough to give yourself the best, which will allow you to give your best to all mankind. On a separate sheet of paper, answer all the questions that follow.

In your own words, define compassion.

Major Players/Situations in My Life

List the people and events that have left a lasting negative impression on you. How and why do you feel that any of the major players/situations left a lasting negative impression on you? What wounds resulted from your interaction with these people or situations?

You can't change what happened, but you can change how you let it affect your present and your future.

Claim Your Victories

What are your accomplishments, the things you do well or are most proud of?

Who are your lifelines and what did they do for you?

Your lifelines are the people who help you along your path. Their contribution may be great or small, but it has had a positive impact on your life. List the names of all of your lifelines and then write what each of them did for you.

What are Your Lessons Learned?

If you're unable to describe something you've learned from experience, then this is a situation that needs deeper exploration. Remember that life is all about progressing from one phase to the next, and if you're not learning, then you're not making progress, which means you aren't living life the way you deserve to.

Example: Today, more and more talented athletes, male and female, are dropping out of college to pursue professional careers in the NBA, the WNBA, and the NFL. Some young adults are choosing to forgo college entirely and stake their claim among the top professional athletes in the United States and the world. The lure of living the glamorous lifestyle of the rich and famous blinds many of these young people to the danger in deciding to pass up their education for fast, easy money — after all, they're doing something they love to do.

Many people nowadays are driven by a need for instant gratification. It never occurs to most high-level athletes that earning a degree first and then having a professional career might be a much better option for the long run. Instead, they choose the pro career now, place the education on hold — sometimes forever — and rarely ask themselves the question "What comes after the glory?"

You rarely hear about the professional athletes who couldn't quite measure up to professional playing expectations and as a result were let go from their teams after a season. Even worse off are the athletes who are injured to the point that their ability isn't what it was. No longer capable of competing professionally, they too are let go. What happens to these people? Sadly, many find themselves average people once again, living in an average world, and working harder than the average person to maintain the lifestyle they became accustomed to during their glory days. Many find it hard to adjust; some find it easier to take their own lives. There is little wonder that athletes rank high in suicide rates: they are unable to handle the pressures of being real-life people.

In the spring of 2005, Shaquille O'Neal finally graduated with a bachelor's degree after taking the time to go back to school. He was reported as saying that it was important for him to have his degree, because when he returned to reality he would have to get a nine-to-five job like so many others. Can you identify the lesson Mr. O'Neal has obviously learned?

Clearly, Shaquille O'Neal realizes that he won't be able to play professional basketball forever; neither he nor anyone else has the ability to play pro ball until they reach retirement age. Therefore, he has to do something else that he does have the ability to do upon retiring from the NBA. Like many smart professional athletes, he will probably become a businessman. However, does being a former pro athlete make him a credible businessman? No! That's why he went back to school to gain the credentials he needed to be a competent businessman. Shaquille might not have learned this lesson from personal experience, but he learned it nonetheless. The good thing is that he learned before it could impact his life negatively.

Learn from your experiences, or someone else's, and you'll find yourself becoming a reflective explorer.

Congratulations — you're on your way!

Living in the Moment

People often make one of two mistakes: instead of living in the present moment, they live in the past or in the future. In either case, if people do not live entirely in the present, something devastating can happen: they lose touch with the reality of what is going on now. The past and the future are great places to visit as often as needed, but are no place to stay. You can't change your past, nor can you be one hundred percent certain that your future will be exactly as you imagine it. The present is the place where you use your past as a tool for achieving your future, whatever you want it to be.

To live effectively in the present, there are certain things you need to know about yourself. Consider the following:

IDENTIFY YOUR CURRENT EMOTIONAL STATE

Are you happy, sad, angry, or apathetic? We all experience these natural emotional states at some point. The important thing to know about them is why you feel the way you do. Are you happy? If so, why? You need to know the answer so you can experience more happiness. After all, happiness is a state of being we all strive to experience.

Anger and sadness, while natural, are emotions that can inhibit your happiness. Holding on to anger is like grasping the handle of a hot frying pan: the longer you hold it, the more it burns and the greater injury you sustain. If, however, you let it go, you experience immediate relief and the healing process begins. If you let go of the anger and other negative baggage you may be carrying, you'll experience relief and open yourself up for the emotional healing process to begin. Anger and sadness can render you powerless to create joy in your life, and unable to make progress.

When we are happy, we are at our best. Happiness is the greatest gift you can give to yourself, and the greatest contribution you can make to mankind. Being happy is an act of love and the most responsible step you can take toward achieving your goals, yet it's the hardest step for most to take. Some people spend their entire lives trying to achieve this emotional state, but their efforts are futile. Why? Because they see what has made someone else happy and they think that same thing will make them happy, too. This is a mistake.

Why is it so important to define happiness for yourself? Though similar in many respects, people have distinctions that make each of us unique, unlike anyone else. Thus you must not assume a universal definition for happiness, because you are unique, and what works for this person or that may not work for you. We all have different interests, values, and circumstances, so we must remember that embracing true happiness comes from the inside out. It's hard to find happiness in ourselves and impossible to find it elsewhere, because, like everything in life, we must define the term for ourselves.

For example, happiness for Michael Jordan may be making millions of dollars and being widely considered the world's best basketball player. If I decide that those very things will make me happy, then I'll never achieve happiness. First, I don't have millions of dollars; second, it's safe to say now that I'll never be considered the world's best basketball player. Clearly, if I base my happiness on what Michael Jordan deems happiness, then I'll never achieve the state of being happy. If, however, I define the term for my circumstances and myself, then happiness will be much closer to my reach, and one day, no doubt, I will achieve my definition of what I believe happiness to be.

It all makes perfect sense if you think about it. Happiness comes from within you; therefore, it is achieved based on your definition of the term. You'll never be able to achieve something that comes from within someone else, because we are all different; there are no replicas. We must take into account those differences in every aspect of ourselves. In the act of learning, we do not all learn the same way, and our educational system must consider that fact to ensure everyone the opportunity to acquire the same knowledge. When we become happy wherever we are presently, the path is clear for us to achieve our goals.

IDENTIFY YOUR STRENGTHS AND WEAKNESSES

You will find that a good businessman who competes daily in our changing economy have the ability to identify the strengths and weakness of his company; as a result, he stays ahead in the global market. You need to know your strengths and weaknesses, because that knowledge will put you ahead in effectively living in the present. Sometimes, we tend to focus more on our weaknesses and fail to recognize our strengths. Conversely, some of us may be so in tune with our strengths that we don't see our weaknesses. Without the ability to identify both, you will not be able to set realistic goals for yourself. As a result, you will probably not develop to your full potential. Moreover, you'll put yourself in a position where lack of knowledge about your strengths and weaknesses will lead you to self-destruction.

Focusing on your weaknesses and ignoring your strengths will make you lack self-esteem, lead an unfulfilled life, and possibly exhibit symptoms of learned helplessness. Focusing on your strengths and being able to identify your weaknesses will result in your becoming a highly confident individual who is able to set realistic goals and achieve them.

No matter who you are or where you come from, you have weaknesses and strengths. Knowing what they are will put you ahead of the game in planning for your future.

IDENTIFY YOUR LEARNING STYLE

Do you know how you learn best? Not knowing your learning style hinders much that you might otherwise learn. There is no universal learning style. We all learn differently, although the education system doesn't always recognize that. The majority of our public schools assume a single learning process for all children. Necessary to this process is the idea that there is one right way to learn, and one "right" or normal mind. As a result, most of the schools in our country value only one type of mind and one type of intelligence.

Howard Gardner, one of the most prominent modern proponents of the concept of multiple cognitive abilities, has developed the theory of multiple intelligences. His theory challenges the notion that there is only one kind of "smart."

According to Gardner, there are at least seven separate intelligences: linguistic, musical, spatial, logical-mathematical, bodily kinesthetic, interpersonal, and intrapersonal. In his observations, schools support the development of only a narrow set of intelligences, thus the majority of Gardner's multiple intelligences go undeveloped. This explains why so many students, both learning disabled and not, fail to realize their full potential.

Even if you're not the traditional student, you still have to know how you learn best. Remember, life itself is an institution of learning. When you stop learning you stop living, so commit yourself to being a 4.0 student of life.

IDENTIFY YOUR INTEREST

We make our present better and more productive by engaging in those activities that we find fulfilling. I encourage you to take risks! Have you ever heard the saying "Nothing beats a failure like a try"? You have to take risks in life; if you don't, you'll never know what you're truly capable of doing.

Wilma Rudolph was a famous track and field athlete who until age eleven could not walk without braces. If she had never tried to run or had accepted her physical circumstances as permanent, then she would never have become the first American woman to win three gold medals in a single Olympics. Had I not risked deciding to be in a regular-education English class, then I wouldn't have known that I was capable of functioning successfully in the regular-education environment.

In taking risks, however, you must know that you will fail sometimes. That is all right. Why? We learn from all our experiences, even the unsuccessful ones. I would venture to say that we learn best from those unsuccessful attempts. As so eloquently told to me by Stephanie Hooks, a teacher in Richmond, Virginia, "Failure cultivates character."

Do you recall when you were first learning to ride your bike without the training wheels? You fell down, right? You may have even hurt yourself, but you got back up, brushed yourself off, and tried again and again until you finally learned how to ride. "If at first you don't succeed, try, try again" is among the best lessons a child could ever learn: perseverance pays off.

Taking risks in life is no different. Anything worth having is worth working for, worth risking. If you have to keep getting back up to do it again and again, so be it. Your future will be all the better because of it.

ACTION PLANNER

Living in the Moment

Self-competence

Self-competence is expert knowledge of one's existence. This is more than merely knowing one's name; competence of self entails being one with mind, body, and soul. Thorough knowledge of one's past, accurate knowledge of one's present emotional, physical, and spiritual state, knowing what one wants out of life, and having a well thought-out course of action to achieve this goal are essential.

What is Your Definition of Happiness?

This definition should be unique to you. If you're truly honest and in tune with yourself, then this definition should never be exactly the same as anyone else's. Using a separate sheet of paper, write your definition of happiness and then answer all the questions that follow.

Describe Your Present Emotional State

How do you feel about your life right now? Are you sad, happy, angry, apathetic? What's making you feel this way? If you're happy, then resolve to do more of the things that make you happy. If you're sad and angry, choose to make a change.

Identify Your Strengths

Your strengths are the things you do well. List them.

Identify Your Weaknesses

Your weaknesses are the things you don't do well. List them.

Explain how you can use your strengths to achieve your goals for the future.

Explain how your weaknesses will hinder your progress toward your goals.

What is Your Learning Style?

Involve your teacher in this process; he or she could be a wealth of wisdom in determining how you learn best. Remember: your present performance in school depends on how much you learn of what your teachers teach. The first step in maximizing your education is being aware of your learning style. Learning doesn't stop for you non-traditional students either, so do your research. How do you learn best? Are you visual, do you prefer to listen, do you like using your hands in the learning process?

What could your teacher do to make learning better for you? Share this with your teacher. Non-traditional students, how can you increase your knowledge?

Name one thing you want to do, but haven't done because of fear, that you're now willing to risk trying to accomplish.

Why are you fearful of trying to do the above?

What will you risk now in order to achieve what you have previously feared?

CHARTING THE COURSE TO NEW HORIZONS

It must be borne in mind that the tragedy of life does not lie in not reaching your goals, the tragedy lies in not having any goals to reach. It isn't a calamity to die with dreams unfulfilled, but it is a calamity not to dream. It is not a disaster to be unable to capture your ideals, but it is a disaster to have no ideals to capture. It is not a disgrace not to reach the stars, but it is a disgrace to have no stars to reach.
— Dr. Benjamin Isaiah Mays

The future is no place to live, but we must visit it often. A life without dreaming, without looking ahead to a better life and imagining how you want things to be for you and your family, is a wasted life. If you're unable to see a future for yourself, then you're more likely to fall prey to life's ills. People who have a clear vision of what they want their future to be are more focused; their plan for their life keeps them protected from the distractions that keep others from reaching their goals.

My life changed forever when I was placed in the special-education program. For a long time, I believed that this change was for the worse, but I now realize that it was the reason for the positive transformations I've made over the years. Not every experience I had in the program was positive, but each one led to a positive outcome. My situation then gave rise to the person I am today — a dreamer, goal setter, and go-getter. Before that placement, I had no direction in life, no dreams, and no motivation; afterward, I unconsciously developed these and a whole lot more.

Dreaming

Like many children, I dreamed quietly. I spent most of each day dreaming. Daydreaming; afternoon dreaming; night dreaming — you name the time, I was somewhere dreaming. Although I felt like a failure, and that feeling soon turned to shame, I knew there was something better in store. Dreaming gave me access to a greater world outside my immediate environment. I started to believe that this greater world was possible when my parents and mentors instilled in me the belief that this world I dreamed of so vividly could one day be my reality.

Daring to dream is the first step to making your dreams into reality. Once you've dealt with your past, identified your present state, and imagined your future, you're ready to chart your course. Envision attaining your dreams and be committed to fulfilling them. Consider it absolutely essential that you pursue your dreams. Jose Ortega y Gasset said, "Human life, by its very nature, has to be dedicated to something." Dedicate yourself to your dreams and make them your reality.

The most wonderful thing about dreaming is that you are limited only by the limits you place on your ability to dream. The world is full of possibilities, and if you believe this to be true, then you know that your dreams are possible.

I challenge you to get a dream, one that you can hold on to. It should be so important and compelling that it wakes you up in the morning and puts you to sleep at night. Your dream should be so vivid that when you contemplate that dream it feels like reality.

I am not talking about having fantasies of winning the lottery or finding a pot of gold at the end of a rainbow or dreaming that you beat Tiger Woods in golf, Michael Jordan in basketball, or Venus Williams in tennis. Those are fantasies, mere wishful thinking. I'm talking about a dream in which, when you envision yourself in the future, you see your best self doing your best work. This type of dream will make you do what's right. It will make you go to school and work and do your best. It will make you respect your teachers and your boss and the knowledge they are trying to impart to you. Having this type of dream will make you move toward achieving your future.

REACHING THE STARS

Have you ever heard the adage "Reach for the stars? I like to think of a dream as millions of stars in a moonlit night. Of course, having immediate access to all these stars would diminish them. If I could simply reach up and snatch them down, I wouldn't be able to observe their full beauty. As a result of reaching them too easily, I would miss some very important details about them; worse, I might not appreciate them as much. My point is that any dream worth reaching will entail challenges that won't be conquered in a day, a week, or a month; sometimes even years won't be enough.

I've been reaching for my stars every since the fifth grade. Since then, I've reached some stars, yet there are many I'm still reaching for. I'm able to try again because I still see the beauty in my dream and I still love my dream.

Michael Jordan's love for his dream of playing basketball was evident at an early age. After being cut from his high school team, he worked harder than ever to make the team the following year.

His love for basketball was even more evident when he quit to play baseball, but then returned to basketball, and when he retired, but returned to play yet again. Michael played basketball less for the fame and fortune than for his love of the game.

When you love your dream, really love your dream, it doesn't matter how many times you reach and miss your stars. You can reach and miss a thousand times, you'll try again a thousand times. It doesn't matter how grand the dream is. It doesn't matter if you want to be a movie star, a teacher, or a truck driver. What matters is that you love your dream with all your heart. Without absolutely loving my dream, I can't imagine working as hard as I do to achieve my goals. And I certainly would never have made it as far as I have.

You won't reach every star you set your sights on — not at first, anyway. There will be challenges, and sometimes these challenges will alter your vision and your ability to see the beauty in your dream. So, it's important that you answer yes to the following:

1. Do you love your dream?
2. Do you have fun pursuing your dream?
3. Are you able to pursue your dream even when you encounter setbacks?

If your answer to any of the above was no, then perhaps you need to rethink your dream. Sometimes our parents, teachers, or others lead us into thinking we want to do this or that when in fact we don't. They're just trying to help, but our dreams must be our own choices. Your dreams are something you have the right to decide at any age.

IF YOUR DREAM DOESN'T MOVE YOU, WHY HAVE IT?

As a teacher and coach, I interact with young people every day. I always wonder which ones will go on to college and become great educators, volleyball players, or both. I wonder which will transform the world, which will be the next Martin Luther King Jr. or Malcolm X.

I've found that it's usually the students with the ability to get right back up after a fall who will be the agents of change, the ones who can take a licking and keep on ticking. They are the ones whose parents, teachers, and coaches don't have to push to get them to study and practice. It's not necessarily the ones with the obvious God-given talent, but the ones with the most self-motivation. Without self-motivation, talent alone is useless.

I didn't know it then, but when I was in school I was full of self-motivation. The young lady I'm about to describe to you, whom I'll call Grace, is an example of someone with all the talent in the world but who lacked the self-motivation necessary to carry her talent to the next level.

Grace and I were born on the same day of the same year and in the same small-town hospital. We grew up only houses away from each other, began school at the same time, and were in the same kindergarten class. We both loved athletics. From eighth grade to our senior year we played the same three sports. Although we had all these things in common, we were entirely different. I actually envied Grace, little knowing that she lacked self-motivation.

Grace was blessed with God-given talent for sports, especially for running. I, on the other hand, was loaded with undeveloped potential. We ran track together and participated in the same events. No mattered how hard I trained, I could never beat Grace at running. Her only area of weakness was the high jump. We both feared it at first, but I figured that if I was ever going to beat her at anything, I would have to get over the fear. I focused my attention on the high jump, which eventually became my strong point.

High jumping requires 10 percent ability and 90 percent technique, so I practiced arching my back when I jumped, and practiced my steps until they were perfect. No matter how often I knocked the bar down, I got back up and jumped again. I kept jumping until I was the top high jumper on my team, first in the district and second best in the region.

Part of me still wanted the glory of being a runner, so I continued training and working on my speed. Whenever I lost a race, I always ran harder in the next race. That's what marked the second difference between Grace and me. I was determined to improve my running, while she was satisfied with not being a competitive high jumper. Eventually, she gave up high jumping altogether. I never gave up running.

By the time we became seniors, Grace had stopped coming to practice on a regular basis; there were even times when our coach had to go to her house and literally pull her out of bed so she wouldn't miss the meet. I guess she figured she didn't need to train because she was the best, and she was right; she was the best at the beginning of our season. By our district meet, however, Grace didn't fare as well. For the first time in four years, I placed second place in the 200-meter dash. Like many other athletes who ran that race, Grace gave up, because she didn't have the endurance to finish the race as strongly as she'd started.

I was officially second best in my district that day, but in my heart I was finally number one. I know I didn't run any faster than I had before, because the same six girls who lost in that race, but advanced to the next level, beat me the following weekend. And when I say beat, I mean beat — I came in dead last! The difference was that they stopped taking their innate ability for granted and did the training necessary to build endurance. My losing was no big surprise: we were all on a level playing field this time; we all started with our best foot forward and finished with our best foot forward, and my best just wasn't enough to win.

Grace believed that physical ability would get her by, but physical ability will only take you so far. Grace took her athletic ability for granted, and became an athlete loaded with undeveloped potential. She, like many teens, didn't realize that even great talent has to be nurtured.

However gifted you are, you still have to nourish your talent and be motivated to strive to reach the next level. There is always a next level, always someone who has the motivation and determination to do what you are doing and do it better. Don't be satisfied with doing the possible; reach for the impossible and you'll achieve it. Dream big and set your goals accordingly. As author Louisa May Alcott wrote, "I can look far away there in the sunshine and see my highest aspirations. I may not reach them, but I can look up and see their beauty, believe in them, and try to follow them."

It doesn't matter who you are, where you come from, how you dress, how you look, how talented you are, or what your social and economic status. We all have the right to dream, and the right and the obligation and the power to actively pursue our dreams.

Dream Haters

Something to keep in mind about dreaming is that not everyone will see your dream as you see it. Some people don't want you to achieve your dream. There are dream haters and dream destroyers in this world. Their mission in life is to help you fall short of achieving your goals. Unable to see the vision you have for yourself, they will list all the circumstances in your life that will prevent you from making your vision into your reality. These are the same people who blame their circumstances for what they are or are not. We must not let the dream haters dictate our dreams and aspirations.

You counteract their negativity by simply holding on to your dreams, even when your circumstances impede them. All great dreamers are encumbered with circumstances that obstruct their dreams. What distinguishes these great dreamers is their ability to hold on to their dreams despite adverse circumstances.

The world is full of great dreamers who allowed their circumstances to determine what they became. People who might have been doctors are drug addicts instead; people who could have been lawyers are criminals; young people who should have been college students are streetwalkers. These people may have had big dreams and hopes, but they let the reality of their circumstances inhibit their dreams to the point where they let them go.

The road to realizing your dreams may be paved with difficulties, but you must keep on dreaming despite them. Others have, and so can you. Mary McCleod Bethune dreamed of opening a school. She only had one dollar. What a challenging situation! Nonetheless, she kept on dreaming, and today, students are being educated at Bethune Cookman College. Stevie Wonder, Ray Charles, and Jose Feliciano all wanted to make music. Each of them was blind, but refused to abandon their dreams, and each became a world-famous composer and performer. If you can keep dreaming despite the adversity you encounter, your dream will eventually overcome your circumstances. It may take longer than you expect, but in the end you will be victorious.

Your past and present do not have to be your future. You alone chart the course of your life, and you can change that course at any time by imagining what you want out of your future, so get busy and start dreaming!

ACTION PLANNER

Charting the Course to New Horizons

Constructivist Living

The constructivist has the ability to adapt to change in everyday life while living life to the fullest. No matter what circumstances arise, the constructivist has the ability to face them head-on with the confidence to overcome. Constructivist living is simply changing as necessary to survive and thrive in the current environment.

What do you dream of acquiring or accomplishing? Close your eyes and imagine your dream, seeing each detail. Are you there? Can you see your dream in all its splendor? Now, open your eyes and, on a separate sheet of paper, write a full description of your dream.

Now, think about how you must change or adapt to your current environment. Write down your ideas and start to make the changes.

Be sure this is *your* dream and not someone else's.

The Final Stop: Make Your Dreams Your Reality!

This is the last stop. You've revisited the past, analyzed the present, and imagined the future. Now it's time for you to start pursuing your dreams.

Goal setting is a powerful technique that can yield strong results in all areas of your life. Setting goals and actively working on achieving them will give you a purpose for taking control of your life, regardless of your circumstances. Like a compass, your goals guide you through life, showing you what direction you need to take. When you are driven by your goals, life has deeper meaning and is more enjoyable. When you have well-developed goals, it's hard for you to be pushed off the path that leads to your dreams.

Prepare Yourself for Your Dream

I have seen many people fall short of achieving their dreams; not because they weren't talented enough or didn't know enough, but because they weren't properly prepared or equipped to succeed. You can take the person out of the ghetto — or out of any other set of circumstances — but that doesn't mean you have taken the ghetto out of the person. There's a great difference between being able to achieve the dream and being equipped to *live* the dream.

How many times have you heard of someone who won the lottery, but a year later is broke and disgusted? They had the dream — the big money — but were not equipped to keep it. You have to be sure that when the day comes that you've achieved your dream, you are able to hold on to it and live out its duration. The following will help you to develop all the skills and characteristics you need to successfully realize your dreams.

Determine Your Motives. One of my goals when I was younger was to go to college and then to law school. The underlying motive was that I wanted my mother and father to realize one of their own goals, which was to see their child achieve more and have more than they had. I can still see my mother's face beaming with pride as she told family and friends, "My baby wants to go to college and become a lawyer."

Although I didn't achieve my parents' goal the way I envisioned it then (and Mom never lets me forget it), I achieved it the way I wanted to: I went to college and chose to become an educator, and I love the choice I made.

Another of my goals is to have children and to see that they have a better life than mine — whatever they choose for themselves — just as my parents envisioned for me. It takes heartfelt intentions like those to provide the motivation you need to make your goals a reality.

Become Disciplined. Talent is helpful in achieving your goals, but talent alone won't make you successful; talent will take you only so far, so it's imperative to develop a work ethic, and that won't happen without discipline.

Discipline is defined as "training expected to produce a specific character or pattern of behavior, especially training that produces moral or mental improvement." Most people are afraid of the word "discipline" because they associate it with control obtained by enforced compliance with strict rules. The fact is people don't like rules!

We want the outcome but we don't want to follow the steps that lead to it. Lack of discipline is a key reason why people fail to realize their dreams. Simply stated, they are not willing to put in the work needed to become and stay successful.

I developed discipline as a middle school student in the special-education program. I remember coming home every day and studying and reading over my notes. I had become so disciplined that my first obligation, even on Fridays, was to study and go over my notes. Faithful to my education, I worked hard to improve, which was one of the main reasons I was able to compete with my regular-education peers.

Discipline is not a once-a-week or twice-a-month thing, but an everyday thing. I had to study every day to become a better student. You have to be disciplined every day to achieve your goals. You have to commit yourself to developing discipline. At first, you might have to force yourself to be disciplined, but it gets easier as time goes on. By the time I got to high school, studying every day was second nature to me. It didn't feel like a chore, it was just part of my everyday living.

Develop Dedication. Have you ever been in a situation where you worked very hard to complete something and, just when you thought you were finished, you realized you weren't even halfway done? Discouraging isn't it? To be able to complete your project at this point you'll need dedication.

Dedication is defined as "complete and wholehearted fidelity." Have you completely committed yourself to achieving your goals and dreams? Will you remain loyal to them even when you encounter setbacks?

I attend a wonderful church with an awesome preacher. One month my pastor taught a series entitled "Developing in the Love of God." His key point was that if you wanted to love perfectly you had to practice loving, which would lead to your becoming developed in love. From his teachings, I learned that what you practice in day-to-day living is ultimately what you become.

Let's say you're the type of person who starts things but never finishes them. In this case, you have committed yourself to practicing quitting, which will make you develop into a quitter. Likewise, if you commit yourself to practicing finishing the endeavors you start, you'll develop into a finisher. It follows that if you practice dedication to your goals and dreams you will eventually become highly developed in dedication, which is crucial to succeeding at setting the goals that will shape your future.

Develop Courage. What keeps you from trying to do things you've never done before? It's lack of courage. I know a bit about this. When I was in high school, my coach said he wanted me to learn to high jump. I was excited until I came face to face with the long, thin, hard bar, which you had to jump over backwards, headfirst. Coach demonstrated, then said, "It's your turn."

I tried to put up a good front. I got into place and ran right up to that bar and looked at it, but my fear wouldn't allow me to even attempt to clear the bar. I just did not have the confidence in my ability to do it. Because I lacked courage, I spent the entire practice running up to the bar without ever trying to jump.

A year later, I said enough is enough. I psyched myself up, dug deep, and found the courage I needed to jump over the bar.

I became the best high jumper on my team. Lack of courage almost prevented me from discovering how well I could actually high jump.

To succeed at anything you must be fearless. Without courage you will never reach your goals, because you'll be too afraid to work toward achieving them.

Be Patient. Choosing your dream is just the first step in making it your reality. Between you and your dream are lots of small steps (goals) you'll have to take. Sometimes there's a long road between the conception of your dream and its realization. During the "between" time you have to develop patience.

Are you patient? Are you capable of calmly waiting for a result without doing anything hasty? If you answered no, then you need to work on your patience.

Most people are not patient. We live in a time when we want everything instantly. We rarely have to wait for anything. Whole dinners can be cooked in minutes thanks to the microwave. But just because we want it right now doesn't mean we always get it right now. Life hardly ever works like that. Sometimes you're ready for change before change is ready for you. During such times, the only thing that can help you is patience.

Patience will prevent you from rushing through life and experiencing burnout. When I was in middle school and throughout high school I developed the belief that I didn't belong in special-education classes. I thrived on winning, making the honor roll, and receiving various awards. After accomplishing one thing, I went right to work on the next, never taking the time to enjoy my accomplishments because I was too busy pursuing what came next.

Take your time. Learn to enjoy the pleasure of achieving the small goals first. It will make you appreciate your dream even more.

Establish Perseverance. Looking back, I realize that my life is a testimony to overcoming setbacks. I was continually getting up and brushing myself off after some event or other. I literally attracted the ground, but I always got back up, most of the time with a smile.

You won't necessarily be smiling after enduing some of life's setbacks. That's all right; just remember to fall on your back, because if you can look up you'll be able to get up and continue toward your goals. The ability to persevere will ensure that you eventually achieve all your goals.

After developing these characteristics, you're almost ready to see your dream through, but there's still some important information you need to know about goals. You have to be able to see your goals clearly and specifically before you can achieve them.

In his book *Live Your Dreams,* Les Brown, the famous motivational speaker who as a child was labeled "mentally retarded," lists a number of goal characteristics. He said that one's goals should be:

- Well defined. You won't know if you've reached them if you haven't established exactly what they are.
- Realistic. Not that you can't be president some day, but shooting for the state legislature might be a wiser first step.
- Exciting and meaningful to you. If your goals aren't exciting and meaningful, where will your motivation come from?
- Locked into your mind.
- Acted upon. There's no sense having a goal if you're not going to go after it.

All those factors are vital to achieving the goals you set for yourself. One of the main reasons why people fail to realize their goals is because they don't set realistic goals in the first place.

A Dose of Reality

My favorite question to ask my high school students is, "What do you want to do with your life?" The responses I get from the majority of my students amaze me. A couple of students said they wanted to be professional football and basketball players. My next question was, "What are you doing to make that happen? Are you currently on the high school team?" They answered no. I then asked them to ponder the likelihood of their playing professional ball if they didn't first play in high school. I also asked them whether they knew of any current professional athletes who hadn't first played ball in high school. They couldn't identify any.

I didn't tell them that their dream was unrealistic. That's a judgment I would never make, even if I thought someone's dream was truly unrealistic. My questioning was intended to make them think and perhaps lead them to a realistic view of their dreams. Its not that they couldn't be professional ball players, but that it's impossible to reach a professional level of proficiency without first practicing and playing in the amateur leagues.

Knowing the importance of goals, I would never undermine anyone's dreams. The mind is a powerful thing, and who am I to say that you can't achieve something? Your goals are your own decisions to make. Nonetheless, there's still something called reality.

Early in my athletic career, I faced something that many student athletes don't face until it's too late: the fact that I would never earn a living at sports; that my role was that of a team player; that I would never be the standout that most of us aspire to be.

I first realized this in the fall of 1992, during girls' basketball season at Southampton High. I thought I was hot stuff, the only ninth grader to make the varsity team and play in the starting lineup. It was the middle of the season and we were doing fairly well. One night, we had a home game against Lakeland High School, which had a very good team. They rarely lost, especially to Southampton. It was a close game to the very end. There were ten seconds left on the clock, we were down by two, and Lakeland was in-bounding the ball from our sideline.

The player in-bounding the ball threw it to one of her teammates. I looked up and saw that the ball was within my reach, so I jumped up with all I had and intercepted it. I don't think I've ever jumped so high. When I came down with the ball, I looked around and spotted our team's leading scorer. I quickly passed the ball. She caught it just behind the three-point line, turned around, and shot the ball just in time to beat the buzzer. She made it!

A wave of people rushed toward me. For an instant, I thought they were coming to praise me for winning the game. Well, they streamed by on both sides, dodging to my right and left in their haste to congratulate the young lady who'd made the game-winning shot.

Hey, I'm the one who stole the ball! I thought. At that moment, on her way to join everyone else, one of my classmates stopped to say, "Good job!" She was the only one who commented on my contribution to winning the game.

That's how much of my athletic career went. No matter what I did, someone else's play always overshadowed mine. The point of the story is that sometimes you just have to face reality.

My reality was not being the star player. The plays I made, though good, weren't the kinds that make you the team star, so I had to reassess my role. I came to the realization that there's only room for a few stars, and that there's nothing wrong with being a team player. You must find and know your place on your team. That doesn't mean you settle for less, but that you don't set yourself up for failure. I made my teammate the star that night. Had I not stolen the ball and thrown it to her, she could never have made the game-winning shot.

From that time, whenever I set foot on any court, I played my best, knowing I'd be contributing to someone else's success. I was able to enjoy what I brought to the game and my contribution to the team. While not a superstar, I knew my play meant something and aided whatever success we had. My athletic goals were simple and clear: I wanted to play my best each time — and I wanted to enjoy playing.

GOAL SETTING

By setting clearly defined goals, you can measure and take pride in achieving them. Actively setting out to achieve your goals allows you to forward progress in what might previously have seemed a long, pointless routine.

Setting goals will enable you to:
- Accomplish more;
- Improve your performance in all you do;
- Build your self-confidence;
- Increase your motivation to achieve;
- Increase your satisfaction in your accomplishments;
- Increase your self-esteem and
- Eliminate attitudes that hold you back and make you unhappy.

Goal setting is a relatively easy process, provided that you know how to set your goals and that you have the self-discipline and dedication to see them through to the very end. Some goals take months or even years to accomplish, and you might have to reassess your goals along the way. Goals are simply road maps that guide you to your dream, and sometimes you have to change direction. It's no problem, as long as you end up where you want to be.

While driving, have you ever had to take a detour because of roadwork? That detour took you off the path you were traveling, but you ended up where you wanted to be, right? In the process of achieving your goals, you'll sometimes have to take a slight detour, but if you're dedicated you'll eventually get back on course.

Staying the Course

The first time I saw Miss Virginia Union University 1996–97, I knew that I wanted to represent my beloved Virginia Union as its queen. At that instant, a dream was born, but just as a newborn baby needs to be nurtured after birth, so does a dream. I nurtured mine by setting goals and developing a plan of action to achieve it.

Always remember, Les Brown said that a dream without a plan is a fantasy. If you're unable to develop a plan of action to make your dream a reality, then your dream will remain just a dream.

Over the next three years, I put my plan into action. I joined several campus organizations, became sophomore class queen, and the following year treasurer of the SGA. It helped a lot that I was already a member of VUU's athletic community. My plan was to become known by my peers as a person with good leadership skills and a glowing love for her university and its administration and staff. I wanted to establish a record of academic excellence, outstanding leadership ability, and service to the university.

At the end of my junior year, I had successfully implemented my plan. My love for the university was evident. There was never any question about my ability to successfully serve as Miss Virginia Union University. My dream became my reality. I was elected Miss Virginia Union University 1999–2000. My theme for the year was "The Dream Precedes the Goal."

Who'd have thought that a little girl from a small town in Virginia, who experienced so much school failure, suffered low self-esteem for years, and had deemed herself stupid and inadequate, would grow to represent a prestigious university with a history of educating some of the world's most prominent African Americans in the fields of theology, political science, education, and many more?

This became my reality because of my ability to dream and to develop a plan of smaller goals that led me to achieving the ultimate goal of becoming Miss Virginia Union University.

Choosing Your Goals

The first step in setting goals is to ask, "What is it that I want to accomplish? What will make me a happier individual, both now and in the future?" Think about your talents, the things that you do best. We all have them; though some are more visible than others, we all have them nonetheless. Using these talents can make your life a lot easier and more enjoyable.

I was still in elementary school when I learned the meaning of the word "talent." I thought that I didn't have one, so I came home from school and asked my mother what my talent was. The question surprised her. She pondered it awhile and then explained, "I'm not exactly sure what your talent is yet, but I know you have one."

"How do you know?" I asked.

"God gives everyone something special that they can do," she replied. "He doesn't always show us what it is when we want Him to. Some people just have to work a little harder to find out what their talent is."

"Well, what can I do to find out what my talent is?"

"You just have to try different things until you find out what it is," she said.

That's exactly what I did. I already knew I wasn't a good singer or dancer, so I tried writing poetry for a while, then drawing. Although I was never satisfied that writing poetry or drawing were my talents, I learned that I could do those things. I've produced some poems and drawings that I was pleased with. Once, I showed one of my pictures to my older cousin, who happens to be a superb artist, and he insisted that I must have traced it. Finally, he conceded, "Cindy, you just might be able to draw." The experience of trying showed me what I was capable of, but I was never satisfied that poetry and art were my talents. I discovered my true talents much later.

The point of my story is that sometimes finding our talents, likes, and dislikes, is all about trial and error, a vital step in setting goals. You'll find some goals much harder to achieve than others, but this doesn't necessarily mean you give up on the hard ones — dreams delayed are not dreams denied.

Start your goal-setting process by developing goals in six areas of life (some may be more relevant then others at this point in your life, but someday they'll all be equally important):

- Family and Home
- Financial and Career
- Spiritual and Ethical
- Physical and Health
- Social and Cultural
- Mental and Education

These areas are connected to each other, ensuring you a well-balanced life. When one or more areas are out of harmony, the entire connection is affected. When you feel stress, it's likely that one of these areas has been thrown out of balance, resulting in disharmony in your life. You must keep each area functioning well to be at your best in day-to-day living. Setting goals in each area will help empower you to achieve your dream.

Ask yourself, "Is anything in the six areas of life holding me back from achieving my dream?" The mental and educational, for example, is an area of life that many people need to work on; most people don't embrace the proper attitude needed to accomplish their dreams. Your attitude, your mindset, is your most precious possession. It determines your success or failure and your happiness or sadness in all that you do.

While in middle school, I developed a love of sports, but a lack of coordination kept me from playing as well as I'd have liked to. When I was first learning to spike a volleyball, my coach had to hold me, tell me when to start my approach, when to jump, and when to swing at the ball. It was really frustrating in the beginning, but in time I mastered the skill. I worked hard to play to the best of my ability. Other people wouldn't always consider my best the best, but I learned to take satisfaction in what I brought to the game. It was attitude that enabled me to do this.

Attitude is everything. Ask yourself, "Is any aspect of my mindset holding me back? Does any of my behavior upset me or keep me from being positive?" If you see yourself as someone who's never happy, if your outlook on life is bleak, or if you let your circumstances dictate the way you react to situations, then your attitude might need adjusting. If so, set goals that will eventually eliminate the problem; perhaps the first goal might be to seek help. Remember, if you think you can or you can't, you're right.

Education is another important area you may need to focus on. Knowledge is a key to living a well-rounded, productive life. We don't all learn at the same rate or the same amount, but every one of us can learn. We should embrace schooling that deals with each of us at our own level of academic function and commit ourselves to learning all we can. Ask yourself, "What information or skill do I need to achieve the goals that I set for myself?" Knowledge is power.

Focusing on the six areas of life will help you set realistic goals that will eventually shape the future you want. On a separate sheet of paper, describe below what you need to improve in each area.

Family and Home
Financial and Career
Spiritual and Ethical
Physical and Health
Social and Cultural
Mental and Education

Now that you've decided what you need to improve, and why, set your priorities by asking yourself, "Which areas need immediate attention, and which ones need the most work?"

For example, if you're still in middle school or high school, finances won't be a high priority for you, because you live with your parents, who are responsible for providing you the essentials. An area such as Mental and Education would have greater priority.

Achieving Your Goals, No Matter What

After deciding what your goals are, you have to set a realistic time frame in which to achieve them. Depending on what you are trying to accomplish, this could be anywhere from an hour to twenty-five years or more.

Let's say you're a ninth grade student and have decided to set goals for the career path you've chosen — becoming a lawyer. A reasonable time frame for this goal would be about twelve years, given that you have three years of high school education left, then four to five years of college, followed by three to four years of law school.

Achieving your dreams can take a very long time, so you can see why patience is so important. Until you get the hang of it, it's best to set goals that you can reasonably expect to accomplish in a time frame of a year or less. Create a plan of action by setting a succession of short-range goals that you'll need to reach along the way to achieving your long-range dream.

ACTION PLANNER

The Individual as Reflective Explorer

Skillful Manager of Everyday Living

The skillful manager is the individual who systematically organizes day-to-day living to produce a desired future outcome.

On a separate sheet of paper, write your dream in the area of family and home.

Now ask yourself:
1. Will my dream enable me to be a better person?
2. Will my dream have a positive impact on others?
3. Am I willing to pay the price of achieving my dream?
4. Can I be confident that achieving my dream will not violate my moral values?

If you answered no to any of those questions, you might want to rethink your dream. Why? Because your dream should:
- always help you to be a better person;

- affect others in a positive way and encourage them to achieve their dreams;
- be something you are willing to struggle for and sacrifice for;
- never make you go against who you are and the values you hold.

Develop a list of three goals that will help get you closer to achieving your dream.

Monitor your goals daily; you might need to make them more challenging or easier to achieve. Ask yourself:

1. Am I making progress toward my goals?
2. Do I still see my dream as clearly as I did in the beginning?
3. Do I still believe in my dream?

If you answered yes to the above, continue on the path to achieving your dream. If you answered no to one or more of the questions, then you need to re-evaluate your goals and/or your dream. Find out why you answered no and make the necessary adjustments.

If you've accomplished your first set of goals but haven't achieved your dream, you must now develop the next set of goals that will get you closer to it. Continue this process until you have realized your dream.

No matter where you are in life, no matter what your circumstances, you are totally equipped to be all you can be, and to make your hopes and dreams become reality. Be fearless in the face of negative circumstances. Don't settle for less. Take life on — live your dream!

By reading this book you've taken the first steps on a journey that will have profound effects on your life. You visited your past, analyzed your present, and imagined your future. Now make it your reality.

Dream Big, for the Dream Precedes the Goal!

ABOUT THE AUTHOR

Cindy Lumpkin- former Miss Metro Atlanta and Miss Virginia Union University is well on her way to becoming a top-ranked motivational speaker and life coach. She has spent the last five years inspiring others to surmount every obstacle that stands between them and their dreams. She has received many honors including being named Outstanding Educator by the Council for Exceptional Children Chapter 077. A Summa Cum Laude graduate of Virginia Union University and a Magma Cum Laude graduate of Clark Atlanta University, she resides in Atlanta with husband, Jason Lumpkin.

Cindy has devoted her life to inspiring and motivating others to overcome life's circumstances. To learn more or for booking information visit: www.triumphinlife.com.

Printed in the United States
132295LV00001B/153/P